T0374718

ANIMUS

Animus

A Short Introduction to Bias in the Law

LEGAL LATIN IN PRACTICE

William D. Araiza

NEW YORK UNIVERSITY PRESS
New York

NEW YORK UNIVERSITY PRESS
New York
www.nyupress.org

© 2017 by New York University
All rights reserved

References to Internet websites (URLs) were accurate at the time of writing. Neither the author nor New York University Press is responsible for URLs that may have expired or changed since the manuscript was prepared.

ISBN: 978-1-4798-4603-0

For Library of Congress Cataloging-in-Publication data, please contact the Library of Congress.

Manufactured in the United States of America

10 9 8 7 6 5 4 3 2 1

Also available as an ebook

For my parents

CONTENTS

Acknowledgments   ix

Introduction: Animus, and Why It Matters   1

PART I. LAYING OUT THE TOOLS

1. Class Legislation and the Prehistory of Animus   11
2. *Department of Agriculture v. Moreno*   29
3. *City of Cleburne v. Cleburne Living Center*   37
4. *Romer* and *Lawrence*   48
5. *United States v. Windsor*   65

PART II. BUILDING THE STRUCTURE

6. What's Wrong with Subjective Dislike?   79
7. Objectively Objectionable   89
8. The Doctrinal Uniqueness of Animus   105
9. The Elusive Search for Animus   120
10. How Much Animus Is Enough? And What Should We Do about It?   134
11. Applying What We Have Learned   144
12. *Obergefell* and Animus   163
Conclusion: Animus Doctrine Today and Tomorrow   173
Notes   181
About the Author   201

ACKNOWLEDGMENTS

One of the many wonderful things about being an academic is that the job description includes, among other tasks, "thinking." This book is the result of thinking about the idea of animus and equal protection law more generally.

Of course, turning thoughts into a book requires more. I have been very fortunate to have that something more. Clara Platter, my wonderful editor at NYU Press, encouraged me to write this book from the moment I mentioned the idea; she and her staff have been unfailingly helpful. Nick Allard, dean of Brooklyn Law School, has supported my writing even during my tenure as vice dean. The professional administrative staff at Brooklyn has also helped, through their enormous expertise and skill in managing the various functions of the Law School, which gave me time to think and write. My husband, as always, has supported and encouraged my writing, even when it has meant late dinners and abandoned evenings.

My academic colleagues, both at Brooklyn and elsewhere, also deserve thanks. In writing this project I've had the benefit of full manuscript reads from both old professional friends (Eric Berger and Joel Goldstein) and new ones (Katie Eyer and Evan Zoldan). Many others have graciously shared their time and insights. Both my husband and Sharon Ben-Meir read the manuscript, to give non-lawyers' perspectives. Thanks to all of you.

I also thank my students. Over the last twenty years I have been fortunate to teach class after class of smart, inquisitive minds. They have asked, pushed (politely), wondered, speculated, and made me look at these ideas with fresh eyes over and over again. If this book reflects worthwhile thoughts, it is largely because my students prompted me to think them.

I owe one final set of thanks—to my parents. They sacrificed to give my siblings and me the opportunities we enjoyed. If they had not made those sacrifices, this book would not have been written.

Introduction

Animus, and Why It Matters

Which of these situations is not like the others?

1. The federal government requires that persons arriving from foreign nations experiencing dangerous outbreaks of communicable diseases go through special screening before entering the county.
2. A state law imposes fines on persons who cross streets without using crosswalks.
3. A town council denies a zoning permit for a group home for intellectually disabled persons, in response to complaints from nearby residents that they don't want "those kind of people" in the neighborhood.

In part, this is a trick question. *Each* of these situations is unlike the others, for different reasons. Most obviously, they differ based on the level of government (national, state, and local) that is acting and the subject matter of the action (public health, traffic safety, and land use). So in a sense, any answer is correct.

But there is an additional axis on which these situations differ—an axis that reflects this book's topic. The first and second situations respond (at least on their faces) to what we can recognize as legitimate health and safety concerns (respectively, public health and traffic safety). (To be sure, such laws could conceivably be "really" motivated by something more sinister, a possibility we will consider later in the book.) By contrast, the facts of the third situation identify a different type of motivation—not a concern for some material public good but, instead, what we can identify for now as the public's simple dislike of a particular group. That situation reflects one version—indeed, the most explicit version—of what constitutional law calls "animus." That's the subject of this book.

Why Does Animus Matter?

At one level, asking why animus matters to constitutional law seems silly. After all, if it is a bad thing for private persons to act out of simple dislike of others, then it should be similarly problematic if government does so. And fundamentally that's right. Indeed, that insight might well strike you as not only right but also important. In other words, among the various differences we can identify between those three situations, this latter difference—the fact that situation number 3 reflects government action taken for a "bad" purpose—may strike us as more profound than the differences concerning which legitimate interest the government is seeking to promote or which level of government is acting.

The intuition that improper government purposes constitute an especially problematic feature of some government actions reflects a great deal of embedded constitutional consciousness. Our constitutional tradition requires that government act only in pursuit of legitimate goals promoting the public good. That's not to say that the Constitution requires that government achieve such goals perfectly. As we know all too well, government often makes mistakes. But it at least has to try. More precisely, government at least has to *seek* to promote a public purpose. Stopping the spread of a contagious virus, or ensuring traffic safety, surely counts as such a public purpose. Harming people just because a political majority doesn't like them does not.

That last insight helps ground in constitutional history our intuition why animus is wrong. The statesmen who gathered in Philadelphia in 1787 to draft our Constitution saw many things wrong with the political order under which they were living. One thing that attracted their particular concern was the tendency of state legislatures to enact legislation impairing traditional contract and property rights. Leaders such as James Madison understood such conduct as reflecting the brute political will of the majority faction in power in a particular state. When that faction took power, he observed, it did all it could to enrich and empower itself, even at the expense of the greater public good.[1]

The Constitution the framers enacted included many features that sought to limit the ability of factions to act purely in pursuit of their own private goals. For now we do not need to worry about those details. But we do need to recognize two basic truths. First, the concern about faction—and by extension, with privately motivated government action—existed from the very start of our constitutional system. Second, and perhaps paradoxically, it was not until the Fourteenth Amendment, ratified in 1868 as part of post–Civil War Reconstruction, that the Constitution gained its most effective tool in combatting such action. In particular, the Equal Protection Clause eventually became understood as a guarantee against the hijacking of governmental power for purely private ends. Such purely private ends include the suppression of a group for no reason other than the fact that the dominant political faction does not like them. Thus the prohibition on animus reflects a core constitutional commitment, one that is most forcefully expressed in the most important constitutional text to have been added since the founding era.

Animus matters more than ever today. At a very practical level, animus has become one of the Supreme Court's favorite tools when considering claims that a plaintiff's equality rights have been violated. As we will see, other approaches to the Equal Protection Clause—in particular, the approach that seeks to determine whether discrimination against a particular group is always suspect and thus always merits more careful judicial scrutiny—have largely run out of steam. Emerging groups—that is, groups whose equality claims have only relatively recently begun to command serious judicial attention—will likely not benefit from such "suspect class" analysis. Indeed, the prime example of such an emerging group—gays and lesbians—has won a remarkable string of equal protection victories at the Court over the last two decades. But those victories have not been won based on suspect class analysis. Instead, they have been won in large part because the Court has found animus.

Animus also matters for a deeper reason. As we all know, American society is more pluralistic than ever; today, Americans hail from more nations, speak more languages, practice more religions (or irreligion), and embrace more different ways of life than ever before. With that diversity has come what one legal scholar has called "pluralism anxiety": that is, a growing cultural discomfort with the extraordinary diversity of contemporary American life.[2] Such discomfort is perhaps natural and, at least, understandable: As enlightened as one might try to be, it takes a great degree of confidence in one's own cultural foundations to accept without reservations persons of vastly differing backgrounds and outlooks. But sometimes that discomfort metastasizes into something more sinister: attempts to legislate social hierarchy by using government power to burden out-groups simply because of who they are. We are right to attach the label "animus" to such actions. But before we do so, we need to make sure we know exactly what we are talking about.

What Does "Animus" Mean?

"Animus" has a lay meaning, partially distinct from its legal usage. In lay terms, "animus" means a strong dislike or hostility.[3] The zoning hypothetical above reflects this meaning: By its terms, the town's zoning decision was motivated by neighbors' desire not live around a certain type of person. But even this common-sense understanding is immediately clouded by ambiguity. There may be lots of reasons people may not wish to live near other types of people. Someone may not wish to live near a fraternity house because the student-residents are prone to playing loud music. Someone else may not wish to live near a family with many children because of the constant activity. Whatever one thinks about the lack of generosity and flexibility inherent in such preferences, we might be willing to accept these explanations as reasonable. But other explanations may not be. For example, we would likely be far less sympathetic to a homeowner's preference not to live next to persons of a different race because he believes them to be sub-human.[4]

The legal definition of "animus" includes this concept of subjective dislike. But it is not enough to simply transfer the concept of private dislike into the context of government action. Part of the problem is that it is hard to reach confident conclusions about the motivations of a government institution such as a town council. Different legislators have different personal motivations; aggregating those motives into a general legislative "will" is a perilous enterprise. And that attempt assumes that it even makes conceptual sense to think of an institution as having an anthropomorphic, subjective will.

To be sure, this is not a conclusive argument against approaching the question of animus by seeking to determine the intent of the government body that took the challenged action. For example, courts that have struggled with the question of governmental intent have recognized that such intent can be implied, or "constructed," by examining more objective criteria. But this difficulty—and, indeed, the response of courts in resorting to more objectively grounded "constructed" intent—does suggest that, when we move past our intuitive understanding of animus toward a legally useful one, we need to move beyond a focus on subjective motivation. As far as constitutional law is concerned, subjective motivation is part of the story. But it is not all of it.

The Outline of This Book

This book examines the constitutional law concept of animus in two parts. Part I consists of several chapters that tell the stories of modern Supreme Court cases implicating animus. The stories in these chapters (Chapters 2–5) play multiple roles. First, they humanize what might otherwise come across as an abstract, theoretical legal question. Second, they illustrate important aspects of what constitutes animus. Finally, and relatedly, they help us piece together the components of a coherent legal doctrine addressing animus.

Chapter 1 is different. Chapter 1 rewinds the clock much farther back—in fact, to the framing of the Constitution in 1787. It explains, in a highly summary form, how the framers expressed the concern we mentioned earlier in this Introduction—the concern about what they called "faction"—that can be understood as the eighteenth-century version of our modern concern with animus. Chapter 1 also explains how in the nineteenth century the concern about faction began to work its way into judicial doctrine through a concept called "class legislation." As one might infer from the label, "class legislation" is a phenomenon in which a private group (a "faction," in the framers' terms) attempts to win the enactment of legislation that aims at enriching or despoiling a particular group (or "class") rather than at promoting the broader public interest. As we will see when we then move on to the cases in Chapters 2–5, this early concern about faction and class legislation echoes distantly, but distinctly, when we examine modern legislation alleged to be grounded in animus.

Together, the cases discussed in Part I provide us with both the raw materials (their fact patterns and conclusions) and the tools (their analysis) that allow us to construct a coherent animus doctrine. This process of construction is a necessary one because the Court has not built that structure itself. Indeed, the cases Chapters 2–5 discuss are often criticized for their extreme opaqueness. Part

II of this book thus takes on the task of using the analysis in those cases to erect the doctrinal structure the Court itself has seen fit to leave unbuilt.

That process begins, in Chapter 6, by explaining how subjective dislike of a group lies at the core of legislation we can legitimately condemn as based in animus. However, it also reminds us of the various problems—both practical and conceptual—that Part I's cases reveal about exclusive reliance on such subjective motivations. Chapter 7 considers what those cases tell us about more objective indicators of animus. As we will see, those indicators themselves reflect another key concept in equal protection law—the concept of discriminatory intent. Chapter 7 explains this concept and notes the clear connection between it and animus.

Chapter 8 considers in more detail the analogy between animus and discriminatory intent. It concludes that, while this analogy clearly exists, an important difference separates the two ideas. As Chapter 8 explains, a finding of animus, unlike a finding of discriminatory intent, ought to end the case. The broader parallel between animus and nineteenth-century-style class legislation supports the argument that an animus finding ought to be fatal to a statute. By contrast, a finding of discriminatory intent, while certainly raising doubts about a statute, only triggers a closer judicial look at the challenged law.

Chapter 9 returns to the question of how to find animus. While Chapter 7 explains how the factors the Court uses to uncover discriminatory intent also help uncover animus, Chapter 8 points out how the animus investigation is slightly different. Borrowing again from the Court's discriminatory intent jurisprudence, Chapter 9 explains how those factors are best deployed to uncover, not discriminatory intent, but the distinct phenomenon of animus.

Chapter 10 tackles the final problem: how conclusive the plaintiff's showing of animus has to be and how persuasive the government has to be when it is put to the test of explaining why its action is *not* based in animus. These are intensely practical questions, but also extremely important ones. Once we address them, we are in a position, finally, to apply the structure Part II creates. Chapter 11 does that by considering several concrete examples in which a plaintiff might credibly claim that she has been the victim of animus-based discrimination.

Chapter 12 considers the final case relevant to our topic: *Obergefell v. Hodges*,[5] the 2015 Supreme Court decision striking down same-sex marriage bans across the nation. While that case did not explicitly rely on the animus doctrine, in a fundamental way it represents the culmination of that doctrine, at least so far in our history. Thus it bears examination for what it reveals about our understanding of animus today. Finally, a brief concluding chapter reflects on how animus doctrine can be a useful tool for courts confronting the widely varying discrimination claims that, more and more, mark our ever-more pluralistic—and thus our ever-more group-identity-conscious—society.

Return now to the question with which this Introduction began. It turns out that the government action in situation number 3 is different from the other two for a very special reason—a reason that is relevant as a fundamental matter of constitutional equality. It is different because the action in that fact pattern is infected with animus. The goal of this book is to figure out what that means.

PART I

Laying Out the Tools

1

Class Legislation and the Prehistory of Animus

By a faction, I understand a number of citizens,
whether amounting to a majority or a minority of the
whole, who are united and actuated by some common
impulse of passion, or of interest, adverse to the rights
of other citizens, or to the permanent and aggregate
interests of the community.
—Federalist No. 10 (James Madison, 1787)

The modern history of animus begins in 1973, with the Supreme
Court's decision in *Department of Agriculture v. Moreno*.[1] Chapter
2 tells the story of that case, with later chapters explaining how the
Court built on *Moreno*'s insights. But *Moreno* itself hearkened back
to earlier insights, even if the Court did not explicitly acknowledge
them. This chapter considers that prehistory.

The Problem of Faction

That prehistory goes back a long way—at least to the era immediately preceding the drafting of the Constitution. During that
time—in particular, the decade between independence and the
Philadelphia Convention in 1787—Americans experienced real
self-government for the first time. At least to some prominent
Americans, that encounter was not unambiguously positive. Soon-
to-be framers such as James Madison observed the tendency of
newly powerful state legislatures to oppress political rivals and
thereby violate rights of contract and property. They noted, for
example, the tendency of legislatures to enact debt-relief legislation

that had the effect of impairing the contractual rights of creditors. Such impairments sometimes took a remarkably targeted form, such as laws that interfered with particular court decisions.[2]

Such violations and interference may be troubling, but what do they have to do with animus? Madison had a theory. Surveying what he had witnessed during that decade-long period, he observed that state legislatures—made newly powerful by the departure of colonial governors and their replacement with often-weaker state governors—had fallen prey to the influence of what he called "faction." In one of the *Federalist Papers*, pamphlets written to persuade New Yorkers to ratify the newly drafted Constitution, Madison defined faction as "a number of citizens, whether amounting to a majority or minority of the whole, who are united and actuated by some common impulse of passion, or of interest, adverse to the rights of other citizens, or to the permanent and aggregate interests of the community." Note that under this definition even a majority can be a "faction"; what distinguishes factions is not their numerosity but their commitment to an interest distinct from the public interest.[3]

Thus Madison assumed that there exist "permanent and aggregate interests of the community," which might be adverse to the interests of even a numerical majority. We can understand such interests, at least conceptually, as those on behalf of the general public or society at large. Of course, this understanding raises the formidable practical challenge of distinguishing factional interests, especially those held by a numerical majority, from such "public" or "general" interests. We will return to that difficulty later in this chapter. But for now we can bracket it, as we examine Madison's theory more fully.

In Federalist No. 10, the same pamphlet in which he identified the problem of factions, Madison explained how the proposed Constitution would limit their power. First, he argued, the system of separated national powers the Constitution established (that is, the executive, legislative, and judicial branches) would help ensure that, at least at the federal level, any particular faction would find it harder to grasp all the reins of sovereign power simultaneously. This argument flowed directly from Madison's observation of state legislatures in the immediate post-independence period. As noted above, that era witnessed more powerful state legislatures, as colonial governors were replaced by often-weaker state governors and as legislatures felt themselves empowered to interfere with judicial decisions. According to Madison, the creation of three independent and co-equal federal branches would help ensure that no faction could easily grasp all the analogous levers of federal power at once.

Second, and sometimes less appreciated, Madison also argued that an "extended" republic[4]—that is, a republic the size of the new United States—was better placed to resist factions. According to Madison, the sheer size of the nation and its government would make it difficult for one particular faction to obtain power in the new federal government. After all, factions, by definition, arose from shared but fundamentally limited interests, such as class interests or particular religious beliefs. Madison's theory is that such factions would naturally be limited in scope—or that, at least, they would find it more difficult to obtain majority support across such a large polity.

But what about states? Madison's innovations applied to the federal government, not the states. Still, the new Constitution spoke to state governments as well. In particular, Article I, Section 10, imposed a list of prohibitions on states. Some of them—for example, the prohibition on states entering into foreign treaties—reflected the necessary transfer of much sovereign power to the new federal government. But more important for our purposes, Article I, Section 10, also included a series of restrictions on states that sought to curb abuses Madison and other framers had detected in states' practices in the then-recent past. In particular, by forbidding states from coining money, making "any Thing but gold and silver Coin a tender in Payment of Debts," or passing any "ex post facto Law" or

"Law impairing the Obligation of Contracts," Section 10 sought to prohibit the particular abuses the framers had detected.

Class Legislation

Still, those and other narrowly focused constitutional prohibitions could not hope to provide comprehensive curbs on state laws that reflected purely private interests, or "factions." The original Constitution was primarily concerned with establishing the new federal government; while the document included scattered limitations on states, state government infringements on liberty and equality were thought to be properly remedied at the state level, by the people of the states themselves. Even the Bill of Rights, which established the familiar catalogue of rights Americans know today (for example, the right to freedom of speech and freedom from unreasonable searches and seizures), was intended to curb only the new federal government. Even as nationalist a jurist as Chief Justice John Marshall admitted as much; in one of his last great opinions he observed that the question of the Bill's application to the states "was of great importance, but of not much difficulty."[5]

Thus, if curbs were to be imposed on factional abuses by state governments, those curbs had to come from states themselves. And indeed, during the first half of the nineteenth century a jurisprudence evolved in state courts that sought to curb such abuses. That jurisprudence sought to police state laws for "class legislation." As one might intuit from the label, "class legislation" was understood to consist of legislation that was intended not to benefit the public or general good but, instead, to enrich or despoil a particular class (or what we might very loosely translate today as an "interest group").

Courts of that era sometimes located the ban on class legislation in specific provisions of their state constitutions. In particular, they often relied on "law of the land" provisions derived from Magna Carta, the thirteenth-century English statement of basic freedoms, which prohibited deprivations of important interests "except by the law of the land." (Tellingly, this phrase was sometimes translated into American state constitutions as "due process of law"—the same restriction that appeared in the Fifth Amendment of the federal Constitution and that would eventually appear in the Fourteenth Amendment as a limitation on state action.) Other lower courts were not so picky about finding a particular textual foundation for their class legislation jurisprudence; sometimes they based their analysis on general, unwritten, principles of republican government.[6]

Regardless of the foundation, the class legislation bar spoke primarily to the generality of the challenged law—whether it prescribed one rule for one group of persons and another rule for another group.[7] The Tennessee supreme court was one of the principal expositors of this idea. As that court explained in an 1829 case, *Vanzant v. Waddell*:

> The right to life, liberty and property, of every individual must stand or fall by the same rule or law that governs every other member of the body politic . . . under similar circumstances; and every partial or private law . . . is unconstitutional and void. Were this otherwise, odious individuals and corporate bodies would be governed by one rule, and the mass of the community who made the law, by another. The idea of a people through their representatives making laws whereby are swept away the life, liberty and property of one or a few citizens, by which neither the representatives nor their other constituents are willing to be bound, is too odious to be tolerated in any government where freedom has a name.[8]

There is deep political theory embedded in this short excerpt. Consider the Tennessee court's concern about what might come to pass if the ban on "partial" or "class" legislation did not exist: In that case, "odious individuals and corporate bodies would be governed by one rule, and the mass of the community who made the law, by another." Such an idea, the court shuddered, was itself "odious." Madison probably nodded with approval at such statements: His concern with factions imposing particularly onerous rules on disfavored groups lay at the heart of statements like the one in *Vanzant*.

One illuminating application of this rule was in another Tennessee case, *Wally's Heirs v. Kennedy*.[9] *Wally's Heirs* was a property law dispute in which the plaintiff sought to eject the defendant from the land in question. The jury ruled for the defendant once the court explained to it a then recently enacted Tennessee law specifying a particular evidentiary rule in land ownership disputes that involved speculative dealings in Indian-owned lands. The Tennessee supreme court reversed the verdict and struck down the law in question, describing it as "peculiarly partial" and "limited in its operation to a comparatively small section of the state, and to a very few individuals claiming a very small portion of the section of country referred to." The court noted that the evidentiary rule at issue, if generally applicable, would defeat the meritorious claims of many bona fide landowners; thinking about the implications of such a result, the court stated that "it is confidently believed such a [generally applicable] law would not have found a single advocate in the legislature."[10]

But the court was not done. It continued:

> The act was intended to drive from the courts of justice a few odious individuals, who it was supposed had speculated upon the ignorance and necessities of the Indian reservees, and fraudulently obtained their claims for trifling considerations, and were corruptly obtaining evidence to establish rights to reserves, where the Indians in fact never had any, to the prejudice of the purchasers from the state. If the supposed facts did exist, there was good cause for public indignation, but none for a violation of the constitution by the passage of a law affecting the rights of a few individuals, but by which the great body of the people, or the legislators themselves,

were unwilling to be bound. The part of the constitution referred to [the Tennessee constitution's "law of the land" clause] was intended to secure to weak and unpopular minorities and individuals equal rights with the majority, who, from the nature of our government, exercise the legislative power. Any other construction of the constitution would set up the majority in the government as a many-headed tyrant, with capacity and power to oppress the minority at pleasure, by odious laws binding on the latter.[11]

So expressed and implemented, class legislation theory could be understood as a powerful, yet restrained, judicial tool. On the one hand, by insisting that laws be general, the prohibition on class legislation ensured fair, non-oppressive, government: After all, as *Vanzant* recognized, nothing stops a majority from enacting oppressive legislation as much as the prospect of that law applying to them as well as their enemies. On the other hand, this tool did not on its face prohibit the government from doing anything, as long as the rules it enacted applied to everyone similarly situated. The self-controlling effect that flowed from forcing the majority to abide by the same restrictions it wished to impose on the minority, remarked upon in *Vanzant* and *Wally's Heirs*, has often been recognized in American law.[12] For example, more than one hundred years after these cases, Justice Robert Jackson of the U.S. Supreme Court recognized that effect when he expressed his preference for using equal protection rather than due process as the primary tool of judicial review, on the theory that, as Jackson said, "the framers of the Constitution knew . . . that there is no more effective practical guaranty against arbitrary and unreasonable government than to require that the principles of law which officials would impose upon a minority must be imposed generally."[13]

We can recognize in this approach the hazy outlines of our modern-day concern with animus. As we will see when we get to modern constitutional law in the next chapter, the Court has consistently stated that "animus," however defined, is a constitutionally illegitimate justification for a legislative action. We can hear a distinct echo of that statement in antebellum courts' insistence that laws not be targeted at minorities simply because they are minorities or simply because they are disliked. The minority in *Wally's Heirs* was clearly disliked; indeed, the court itself described them as "odious." But to single them out for a burden—in the words of *Wally's Heirs*, "to drive [them] from the courts of justice"— simply because they were disliked was constitutionally inadmissible. Under the Tennessee constitution's law-of-the-land clause, it seemed, everyone—including despised minorities—enjoyed the right to be governed by the same law.

Still, the class legislation idea was difficult to apply. It might be fine in theory to insist that laws be general and that political majorities apply to themselves to same laws they wish to apply to minorities. But what if the situation genuinely called for differential treatment? Consider again the facts of *Wally's Heirs*. The targeted group was apparently "odious" for a reason: Even the court that ruled in their favor recognized that they had preyed on Indian landowners ignorant of their legal rights and had "fraudulently" obtained land claims "for trifling considerations," and "were corruptly obtaining evidence to establish" their legal rights. Would those concerns justify a law that imposed special evidentiary burdens on them? And what if the legislature had not explicitly stated that these were the reasons for imposing those burdens? Would a court be justified in speculating that a legitimate justification might have motivated the legislature? It was with these difficult issues that the federal courts, and the Supreme Court in particular, had to begin wrestling after 1868, when the Fourteenth Amendment constitutionalized the rule against class legislation.

Fourteenth Amendment Class Legislation Jurisprudence

There is no doubt that the Fourteenth Amendment was primarily intended to address the inequality and rights deprivations suffered by the newly freed slaves and by African Americans, more generally. Nevertheless, the drafters and backers of the amendment just as clearly intended its beneficial effects to extend beyond the newly freed slaves, African Americans, and even racial issues, more generally. Indeed, the legislative history of the amendment contains explicit references to class legislation and assurances that the amendment would outlaw caste systems.[14]

But despite its promised impact (or perhaps because of it), the Supreme Court approached the amendment warily. In 1873 it gave a narrow reading to what many legislators then (and many scholars now) considered its most important substantive rights provision—the Privileges or Immunities Clause of Section 1.[15] *The Slaughter-House Cases*[16] involved a Louisiana law that established a monopoly slaughterhouse in New Orleans, which allegedly infringed on the rights of the city's butchers to ply their trade. The plaintiffs recognized that the state enjoyed great latitude to regulate private enterprise for the health and safety of the citizenry—here, the health of New Orleanians, which might be compromised, for example, by the location of slaughterhouses near the city's drinking water source.[17] But they—and the *Slaughter-House* dissenters— insisted that Louisiana's grant of a monopoly to one slaughterhouse company was unrelated to such public needs. Their argument echoed pre-war class legislation arguments: The monopoly, they insisted, reflected nothing but a simple preference for one group of citizens (the holders of the monopoly) at the expense of another (the butchers who could no longer ply their trade freely). The majority, however, concluded that the Fourteenth Amendment did not impose stringent restrictions on state actions of this sort, mainly by reading the Privileges or Immunities Clause exceptionally narrowly—wrongly so, in the view of most modern scholars.[18]

As a case that was not about race (the obvious main focus of the amendment's drafters), one might dismiss *Slaughter-House* as an unreliable indicator of the Court's attitude. However, two years later, in *United States v. Cruikshank*,[19] the Court threw out a federal indictment alleging that whites who had massacred a group of blacks as the culmination of a political feud had violated the blacks' civil rights. In doing so, the *Cruikshank* Court expressed a highly constricted reading of the rights granted by the Fourteenth Amendment, in a context that would appear to implicate the core of the amendment's intended operation. Sadly, *Cruikshank* was not an anomaly; by the early 1880s the Court had largely (though not completely) turned its back on aggressive enforcement of the amendment's racial equality promise.[20]

Despite these setbacks, the Court soon set about to employ the Fourteenth Amendment as a tool to rein in overly aggressive state regulation. However, it did so not in the racial area, where, for the most part, the Court was to remain disturbingly quiescent for nearly two generations, but rather in the area of state regulation of the economy. In beginning down this new jurisprudential path, the Court began employing the rhetoric of class legislation.

Consider, for example, *Barbier v. Connolly*.[21] *Barbier* is known today as a precursor to the much better known case of *Yick Wo v. Hopkins*.[22] Both cases dealt with fire prevention legislation in San Francisco, which limited the operations of laundries in order to prevent fires. While *Yick Wo*'s strike-down of that legislation is widely understood today as an early example of the Court's (intermittent) concern with racial discrimination, *Barbier*, a case shorn of any obvious racial component, is notable for its statement of the class legislation idea, as transplanted into the Fourteenth Amendment. Justice Stephen Field wrote the following for the Court in *Barbier*:

> The fourteenth amendment, in declaring that no state "shall deprive any person of life, liberty, or property without due process of law, nor deny to any person within its jurisdiction the equal protection of the laws," undoubtedly intended not only that there should be no arbitrary deprivation of life or liberty, or arbitrary spoliation of property, but that equal protection and security should be given to

all under like circumstances in the enjoyment of their personal and civil rights . . . ; that no impediment should be interposed to the pursuits of any one, except as applied to the same pursuits by others under like circumstances; [and] that no greater burdens should be laid upon one than are laid upon others in the same calling and condition. . . .

But neither the amendment . . . nor any other amendment, was designed to interfere with the power of the state, sometimes termed its police power, to prescribe regulations to promote the health, peace, morals, education, and good order of the people, and to legislate so as to increase the industries of the state, develop its resources, and add to its wealth and prosperity. From the very necessities of society, legislation of a special character, having these objects in view, must often be had in certain districts, such as for draining marshes and irrigating arid plains. Special burdens are often necessary for general benefits,—for supplying water, preventing fires, lighting districts, cleaning streets, opening parks, and many other objects. Regulations for these purposes may press with more or less weight upon one than upon another, but they are designed, not to impose unequal or unnecessary restrictions upon any one, but to promote, with as little individual inconvenience as possible, the general good. Though, in many respects, necessarily special in their character, they do not furnish just ground of complaint if they operate alike upon all persons and property under the same circumstances and conditions. Class legislation, discriminating against some and favoring others, is prohibited; but legislation which, in carrying out a public purpose, is limited in its application, if within the sphere of its operation it affects alike all persons similarly situated, is not within [*i.e.*, not prohibited by] the amendment.[23]

In this statement we can find the theory of the class legislation prohibition, the assurance of its limited scope, and, finally the challenges that would ultimately cause the Court to abandon it.

First, the theory: As Justice Field explained in the first paragraph of this excerpt, the Fourteenth Amendment aimed at, among other things, ensuring that legislation would apply equally to all—"that no impediment should be interposed to the pursuits of any one, except as applied to the same pursuits by others under like circumstances." Second, he stated the assurance, in the second paragraph, that the amendment did not strip states of their power to regulate for the general good—a power called throughout this era "the police power" (although it extended far beyond what we know today as modern policing, to include all regulation for the health, safety, and prosperity of the community).

Third, the challenge: Justice Field—a jurist notable for his insistence on protecting business and entrepreneurs from what he deemed unnecessary or unfair regulation—nevertheless recognized that sometimes government was justified in imposing regulations that imposed burdens on some groups but not others. As he put it, "Special burdens are often necessary for general benefits"; he then gave a series of examples that would have spoken to his nineteenth-century audience. But what then of the bar on class legislation? Recall his response: "Class legislation, discriminating against some and favoring others, is prohibited; but legislation which, in carrying out a public purpose, is limited in its application, if within the sphere of its operation it affects alike all persons similarly situated, is not within [that is, not prohibited by] the amendment."

Thus "special burdens" were not unconstitutional, as long as they were "necessary for general benefits" or for "carrying out a public purpose" and as long as "within the sphere of [their] operation [they affect] alike all persons similarly situated." But that last phrase carries with it the seeds of the difficulty that would bedevil courts as they scrutinized state laws for unconstitutional class legislation: How would one know if the persons affected really were "similarly situated"? Return to the antebellum Tennessee supreme court opinion in *Wally's Heirs*. The court there described the group subject to the burdensome evidentiary rule as "odious," as having engaged in fraud and speculation that capitalized on the legal ignorance of Indian landowners. Today, most of us would find such persons not similarly situated to everyday, law-abiding landowners seeking to preserve their property rights in court. The court in *Wally's Heirs* thought the answer was so clearly contrary to that intuition that it did not feel the need to provide an extended discussion of the point.

Let us now update our facts seventy years past *Wally's Heirs*. In 1897, the Court decided *Gulf, Colorado, & Santa Fe Railway v. Ellis*,[24] striking down a Texas law making railroad company defendants liable for attorney's fees in small-amount lawsuits. The Court could find no reason to single out railroads for that burden. Yet two years later, in *Atchison, Topeka, & Santa Fe Railroad v. Matthews*,[25] the Court *upheld* a Kansas law that made railroad defendants liable for attorney's fees in cases arising out of fires caused by railroad operations.

Why these two different results? Of course, we have our intuitions: In the nineteenth century the sparks from trains often caused fires. But that just begs the question why *those* fires were more problematic, or blameworthy (or whatever), as to justify the attorney's fees rule when the Texas law singling out railroads was held to classify arbitrarily. This is not to suggest that these cases are irreconcilable; again, it is easy to point to the relationship between railroad operations and fire danger and recognize the connection. But intuitions are not legal principles, unless we are content with having courts reweigh whatever intuitions or value choices legislatures made when enacting these laws in the first place. (Remember, the Texas legislature presumably thought that in the area of small-amount lawsuits there was also something about railroads that justified deviating from the normal attorney's fees rule.) To repeat, maybe *Ellis* and *Matthews* are irreconcilable. Maybe they are not. But in a deeper sense, that unpredictability is exactly the point.

This unpredictability infected judicial review of every statute dealing with what we now call "social and economic legislation," that is, legislation regulating economic and social relationships between different groups. Without guidance on *how carefully* to review such legislation, courts were left to their own intuitions about which laws imposing "special burdens" were really doing so in pursuit of obtaining "general benefits" and which legislation really was "class" legislation. The Court did not suggest a potentially enduring resolution of this problem for another generation after the railroad cases—that is, until 1938.

Carolene Products

A lot of constitutional law was made in 1937 and 1938. The Court turned away—decisively, it turned out—from according careful protection to a right the Court had previously found in the Due Process Clause, the so-called "right to contract."[26] At the same time, it turned away—again, ultimately decisively—from imposing artificial restraints on Congress's ability to regulate interstate commerce.[27] Beyond smoothing the path for increased federal regulation of the economy, these cases (and others)[28] greatly altered the role of the federal courts in our governmental system.

One decision from those two years did not immediately change the courts' role but only hinted at such a change. By 1938, *United States v. Carolene Products*[29] was a run-of-the-mill case. It involved the Carolene Products Company's challenge to a federal law banning the interstate shipment of "filled milk," a foodstuff that resembled milk but was, rather than pure milk, a combination of milk combined (or "filled") with other fats. The company's claims—that Congress lacked the power under the Interstate Commerce Clause to regulate the interstate shipment of that product and that, even if it possessed that power, the Fifth Amendment's Due Process Clause protected the company's right to contract to sell that product—were both easily answerable by 1938, in favor of congressional power to enact the statute and against the firm's alleged right to contract.

But in the course of repeating what by then had become the established law that courts would presume that facts existed justifying such economic regulation, four justices of the Court waded into new waters. Speaking through Justice Harlan Fiske Stone, those four justices suggested in Footnote 4 of the opinion that such deference might not extend to certain situations: when a law appeared to violate one of the Bill of Rights, when a law restricted access to the political process (such as a law restricting voting or speech rights), and, most relevantly for our purposes, when "prejudice against discrete and insular minorities" (eventually known as "suspect classes") had the effect of creating a dysfunctional political process.

That last part of the footnote—the famous "Footnote 4" of the *Carolene Products* opinion—became the foundation for what became known as the Court's "suspect class" jurisprudence. That jurisprudence sought to identify certain types of discrimination that merited heightened scrutiny because of the nature of the group suffering the discrimination. Starting in the late 1960s the Court, and sometimes particular justices, employed suspect class analysis to argue for heightened judicial scrutiny of discrimination based a variety of other characteristics, such as sex, alienage, and illegitimacy.[30]

The story of suspect class analysis, and its ultimate fate, is far too intricate to consider in detail here, although later chapters will discuss both it and its relationship to animus. For now, it suffices to note that suspect class analysis offered a methodology for determining when a court should give careful scrutiny to a law that was alleged to violate equal protection. Recall that up to that point the Court had attempted to answer such questions by determining whether the law constituted illegitimate class legislation rather than an effort to further a legitimate public interest. Recall also that that task required courts to determine whether differently treated parties really were similarly situated. Such determinations were difficult, as suggested by the two railroad cases from the end of the nineteenth century. They required courts essentially to re-weigh the policy and value choices legislatures had made when enacting the challenged law.

Suspect class analysis attempted to avoid that difficulty, by helping courts determine when legislative classifications were so inherently "suspect" that they merited closer attention. If a group was deemed not to be the victim of "prejudice," and thus not to suffer from the political exclusion Footnote 4 described, then courts should presume that that group could advocate for its in-terests in the political process and thus avoid legislation that un-fairly or arbitrarily singled it out. In such a case the court would give only the most deferential scrutiny to legislation burdening that group. Today, that deferential review is known as "rational basis" review, which asks simply whether the legislature had a rational basis for believing that the challenged classification was related to the promotion of a legitimate government interest. As we will see when we get to the modern law, today rational basis review is usually exceptionally deferential, and usually—though not always—results in a win for the government. But if a group *were* the victim of such political exclusion—or, to use modern terminology, if governmental classifications on that ground were considered "suspect"—then Footnote 4 implied that more careful judicial review would be called for. Today, we call such review "heightened scrutiny."

This theory of judicial review promised a neutral justification for judicial review, based solely on whether the political process was functioning properly. As such, it offered an escape from the trap the Court had set for itself, in which its attempts to ensure that laws pursued legitimate public purposes inevitably ensnared it in a second-guessing of legislatures' substantive policy judgments. We can thus understand the revolutionary potential of Footnote 4's theory, still embryonic in 1938.

It took several decades before Footnote 4's implications blossomed into what we now know as suspect class analysis. Unfortunately, after about a decade and a half of experimentation beginning in the late 1960s, the suspect class enterprise encountered insurmountable conceptual and practical difficulties. As Chapter 3 will explain, one of the Court's responses to the breakdown of suspect class analysis was to return to the class legislation era's more granular, case-by-case approach for determining when a challenged law really did pursue a valid public purpose and when it did not. But the modern incarnation of that form of judicial review involved a new consideration: an examination of whether the challenged law was motivated by animus. As we will see in the next chapter, the foundation for such an approach was provided by a seemingly odd little case from 1973, ironically, just as the Court was beginning to embrace suspect class analysis.

Coda: Class Legislation in Retrospect (and Prospect)

In retrospect one can understand why the class legislation concept faded into history. Any doctrine that required courts to scrutinize carefully whether a law was intended to promote a legitimate public interest but that recognized that such public interests could be promoted by laws that treated different groups differently would inevitably embroil courts in second-guessing either legislatures' intentions and/or the efficacy of legislation in promoting the public good. The expanding need for regulation of all sorts that accompanied the industrialization of America meant that occasions for this type of judicial review would arise repeatedly.[31] Given all this, one can understand why Justice Stone in *Carolene Products* announced his rule deferring to legislative judgments that a given law promoted the public good. With that deference necessarily came an end to the era of meaningful class legislation scrutiny.

Nevertheless, modern scholars of vastly different stripes have rediscovered the class legislation idea. Those who doubt the staying power of *Carolene Products*–inspired suspect class theory have called for a renewed focus on class legislation.[32] Similarly, scholars who believe that legislatures habitually cater to entrenched economic interests that prefer a regulated market excluding new competitors have cited the class legislation idea that government should not favor the rich and powerful but should regulate evenhandedly.[33] Others, who argue that equal protection is fundamentally a rule, not about proper classification, but instead about ensuring that no group is subordinated, have also found support in the class legislation concept, which they see as a rule against such systematic subordination.[34] Finally, political theorists have rediscovered in the class legislation concept a political theory that seeks good governance by requiring that the majority be willing to live by the same rules they impose on disliked minorities, just as the Tennessee supreme court insisted in *Vanzant*, nearly two hundred years ago.[35] Supporting these arguments is the claim that any doctrine that, like class legislation, has such a strong historical pedigree is worthy of consideration as an appropriate interpretation of the Equal Protection Clause, especially given the interpretive difficulties otherwise raised by the clause's open-ended character.

To be sure, as we noted above, a return to the class legislation era remains problematic to the extent that it implies potentially intrusive judicial review of legislative policy making. It is also likely implausible, given the current Court's continual insistence that it has no wish to return to the pre–*Carolene Products* era of judicial review. But what *is* possible is a resurrection of the *principle* of class legislation—the principle that prevents political majorities from burdening minorities without any good reason.[36] What follows in this book is an argument that that underlying principle can be found, if one looks hard enough, in the doctrine of animus.

2

Department of Agriculture v. Moreno

[I]f the constitutional conception of "equal protection of the laws" means anything, it must at the very
least mean that a bare congressional desire to harm a
politically unpopular group cannot constitute a legitimate governmental interest.
—*Moreno* (1973)

In some ways, *Department of Agriculture v. Moreno*[1] sounds odd
to modern ears. The case, decided in 1973, features congresspersons' verbal attacks on "hippies" and "hippie communes," terms
that call to mind the counterculture of the 1960s and mainstream
America's reaction to it. But the Court's holding in that case—that
a desire to harm those persons could not support the constitutionality of Congress's action—survived the fading of the Flower Power
era. *Moreno*'s famous statement about bad legislative motive—the
phrase quoted at the start of this chapter—has been cited consistently by the Court over the subsequent forty years when a statute
appeared to the Court to be grounded in animus. In a very real way,
that statement has become the foundation of the modern Court's
animus doctrine. For that reason *Moreno*, despite its anachronistic
facts, merits a close look.

Moreno's Facts

For a case supposedly about hippies, the plaintiffs in *Moreno* were
remarkably mundane. For example, the named plaintiff, Jacinta
Moreno, was a fifty-six-year-old woman living in Homestead,

Florida, who suffered from diabetes and moved in with her neighbor and her neighbor's three children in order to make ends meet. Her lawyer's description of her economic situation features the telling details of someone just getting by: a public assistance income of $75 per month, out of which she spent $40 as her share of the joint rent, $10 for her share of the gas and electric, $10 for bus fare for her monthly trips to the hospital, and $5 for laundry—leaving $10 for her food budget, supplemented by food stamps.

Sheila Ann Hejny, of Kernersville, North Carolina, faced a different type of challenge. She, her husband, and their three children were also impoverished and thus also received food stamps. Their legal situation changed when they took in a neighbor's child who had been forced to leave her home. According to Ms. Hejny's lawyer, the young girl had shown a great deal of behavioral improvement since moving in with the Hejny family.

These were two[2] stories that were in many ways different. But they were similar in that they both reflected persons struggling to get by and doing so in part by living in households that were at least slightly unconventional, in the sense that they included unrelated persons. That's where the problem arose. In January 1971, Congress amended the federal food stamp program to change the definition of "household," the unit by which food stamp eligibility had customarily been determined. As translated into regulations promulgated by the Secretary of Agriculture (the agency in charge of the food stamp program), the amendment meant that, with minor exceptions, a group of persons living together could not qualify for food stamps if the home included unrelated persons "living as one economic unit sharing common cooking facilities and for whom food is customarily purchased in common."[3] Thus neither Jacinta Moreno, living with her neighbor, nor Sheila Ann Hejny, whose family had taken in their neighbor's daughter, remained eligible to receive food stamps.

Moreno in the Courts

When the *Moreno* plaintiffs sued in federal district court, the government argued that the law satisfied the "rational basis" test, which Chapter 1 sketched out in its conclusion.[4] Logically enough, the lower court began its equal protection analysis by considering the overall purposes of the food stamp program, stated in the statute: to alleviate hunger and malnutrition and improve the agricultural economy. But it could find no rational connection between the household definition statute and those goals.

Turning away from the statute as a whole and toward the challenged amendment itself, the lower court could find no possible rationale for the law except "to combat the unconventional living arrangements popularly associated with" hippies. But it refused to accept that justification as adequate, on two grounds. First, it noted then-recent Supreme Court precedent protecting rights to free speech and intimate association and questioned whether this potential justification for the food stamp amendment could survive the Court's protection of such privacy rights, given how the law penalized certain lifestyle choices. Second, it concluded that, even if the morality justification could survive constitutional scrutiny, it would be overbroad, since the law penalized all living units including unrelated persons—not just such units that were composed of persons of both sexes. (Apparently, the possibility of same-sex intimate relationships did not even cross the court's mind as something that Congress might have been thinking of trying to penalize as immoral!) Based on this reasoning the lower court held that the amendment violated the Constitution.

On review, the Supreme Court affirmed the lower court. The Court began by repeating the lower court's conclusion that the household definition law did not rationally further either of the food stamp program's overall goals. It then sought to determine the law's possible goals by referring to the legislative history. As the introduction to this chapter implied, that legislative history, though sparse, included references to "hippies" and "hippie communes" as the intended targets of the newly limited "household" definition. It was those references to Congress's purpose that led the Court to state that "a bare . . . desire to harm a politically unpopular group" could not serve as a legitimate government interest motivating a law.

At the Supreme Court, the government apparently changed its approach from its litigation in the trial court, "abandon[ing]" the morality argument but offering other interests instead: the increased potential for abuse of the program posed by households of unrelated individuals and the relative instability of such households, thereby "increasing the difficulty of detecting such abuses."[5] The Court then proceeded to consider those interests. But before we turn to that consideration, let us see where the Court's analysis had taken it so far. At this point in the opinion, the Court had agreed with the lower court that the household definition law had no rational connection with the overall purposes of the food stamp program. It had then cited the legislative history about "hippies" and "hippie communes" and concluded that a desire simply to harm those groups did not constitute a legitimate purpose.

In other words, then, the Court had examined both sides of the rational relationship test and found the challenged law to be deficient. When considering the food stamp statute's overall goals it found no connection to the household definition law. But when it then looked further and examined the goals that *did* appear to motivate Congress, it found those goals inadmissible—indeed, illegitimate. With no connection to the goals that ostensibly motivated the food stamp law as a whole, and with goals that did in fact seem to motivate Congress condemned as illegitimate, it is no surprise that the Court approached the government's argument with skepticism.

Given that understandable skepticism, the Court made short work of the anti-fraud rationales the government offered. It noted that other provisions of the food stamp law addressed that concern, a fact that was enough to cast "considerable doubt" on the government's explanation. Even more damningly, however, it explained that the household definition statute was almost laughably irrational in addressing that concern. It explained that, under that statute's definition, a "household" constituted persons who (1) lived as "an economic unit," (2) shared "cooking facilities," and (3) "for whom food is customarily purchased in common." Thus, Justice Brennan explained, two unrelated persons who wanted to both collect food stamps could simply set up two "households," say, by buying their own food, setting up separate cooking facilities, or otherwise not living as "an economic unit"—for example, by paying their own bills.

Of course, such steps would require financial resources. Ironically, then, truly indigent persons—people like Jacinta Moreno—would find it harder to circumvent these requirements than poor, but not destitute, people who could, for example, buy their own food and thus qualify as two separate households under one roof, each of which would continue to be eligible for food stamps. As Justice Brennan put it, "[I]n practical operation, the 1971 amendment excludes from participation in the food stamp program, not those persons who are 'likely to abuse the program,' but, rather, only those persons who are so desperately in need of aid that they cannot even afford to alter their living arrangements so as to retain their eligibility." He conceded that "[t]raditional equal protection analysis does not require that every classification be drawn with precise 'mathematical nicety.'" "But," he concluded, "the classification here in issue is not only 'imprecise,' it is wholly without any rational basis."[6]

To be sure, Justice Rehnquist, joined by Chief Justice Burger, disagreed, finding that the statute did satisfy the minimum level of rationality review the court required.[7] In particular, he concluded that the household definition statute was, as he put it, "not . . . quite as irrational as the Court seems to believe" as an anti-fraud measure. Hardly a vote of confidence but, nevertheless, he concluded, enough to sustain the statute, given the great degree of deference that characterizes traditional rational basis review. Notably, he did not discuss the legislative history indicating a more sinister—and, in the majority's view, constitutionally illegitimate—motive.

Justice Rehnquist's argument demands engagement. After all, he is right—and indeed, the majority conceded—that rational basis review does not ask much of the government. Perhaps the claimed anti-fraud/fraud detection concerns *were*, if nowhere near a perfect match for the statute's household definition, at least close enough to justify their upholding. Why, then, did the majority apply (at least somewhat) elevated scrutiny? As we will see in later chapters, this is in many ways the fundamental question of rational basis review. Those chapters will discuss government actions—a city council's land-use decision, a voter-enacted state-law initiative, and a federal statute—that were all defended as promoting reasonable-sounding justifications. None of those actions promoted those legitimate interests with laser-like precision. But, as each of these government defendants (accurately) noted, rational basis review does not require such precision. Nevertheless, the Court struck all of them down, finding animus. How did it do so? What is the relationship between irrationality and animus? We begin this discussion with *Moreno* because it is the foundational modern case for examining that relationship.

Irrationality and Animus in *Moreno*

Let's return to the majority's analysis. Recall that the Court began, reasonably enough, by considering the explicitly stated goals of the food stamp program: alleviating hunger and promoting the agricultural economy. As the Court noted, the household definition statute played no role in furthering those goals. To be sure, that fact should not necessarily give rise to suspicion that the statute sought to further illegitimate goals or that the statute lacked any rational connection to a legitimate government interest. After all, we can imagine many pieces of the food stamp regime that probably do not directly further those goals. Indeed, any restriction on the availability of food stamps would presumably fall into that category. This should not be surprising: Small, detailed parts of a complex statute often promote its general goals only indirectly, as part of an interlocking scheme of provisions. Asking that each such component directly promote the broad, overall goals of the statute is often asking too much.

But there was more. After finding no close (or even rational) connection to those broader goals, the Court examined the household definition statute in more detail, to discern what Congress might have intended more particularly. That investigation revealed real trouble signs—the legislative history revealing Congress's punitive motivations. Of course, those motivations could not suffice to uphold the statute. Thus, the Court turned to the statute's last defense—the anti-fraud justifications that the government's lawyers suggested might have justified the law. Justice Rehnquist found those justifications adequate. But he did so in a vacuum—that is, without acknowledging the previous steps the majority had taken.

Doing our best to reconcile the majority and dissenting opinions leads us to the conclusion that that background context—the statute's lack of connection to the broader goals of the food stamp program and the troubling character of its more particularized motivations—must have made a difference. In particular, one can perhaps understand the majority's reading as follows. First, any statute must have a purpose against which it has to be tested for fit, even if that test is deferential (as the rational basis standard is). With the food stamp program's more general goals discounted as possible purposes, the Court might then have reasoned that the statute needed to stand or fall on grounds particular to it. But the most obvious of those grounds—the purpose expressed by the legislative history—was not adequate. Indeed, it was worse than inadequate: As later courts would suggest, it was affirmatively problematic.

Still, the *Moreno* Court itself did not characterize that purpose in those terms. Indeed, in the sentence immediately following its soon-to-be famous statement about "a bare desire to harm" not "constitut[ing] a legitimate government interest," the Court, quoting the lower court, then said the following: "As a result, '(a) purpose to discriminate against hippies cannot, in and of itself and without reference to (some independent) considerations in the public interest, justify the 1971 amendment.'"[8] Note what that sentence says: "[A] purpose to discriminate against hippies" cannot justify the household definition statute "in and of itself and without reference to (some independent) considerations in the public interest." Thus the Court did not stop its analysis when it uncovered the legislative history suggesting that the household definition statute was motivated by "a bare desire to harm" hippies and hippie communes. Instead, it pressed on, which meant examining the government's proffered anti-fraud justification.

But by this time the Court was rightly suspicious. The statute did not further the food stamp program's overall goals. And the statute's most evident goal was inadmissible and constitutionally troubling. And finally, the government had come up with the anti-fraud goals well after the fact.[9] With poorly fitting goals, concocted long after the fact, standing in for the apparently actual (but illegitimate) goals of the statute, and with the statute not even close to fitting the overall program's goals, it should not surprise us that the *Moreno* Court found a constitutionally inadequate fit, even given its concession that the rational basis standard did not require "mathematical nicety." Justice Rehnquist mentioned none of this.

To be sure, the *Moreno* majority did not lay any of this out. But it did establish the groundwork for the evolution of animus doctrine, through both its famous statement about "a bare desire to harm" constituting an illegitimate government purpose and its skeletal application of that principle. It would fall to later cases to flesh out the implications of its analysis.

3

City of Cleburne v. Cleburne Living Center

> The short of it is that requiring the permit in this case
> appears to us to rest on an irrational prejudice against
> the mentally retarded.
> —*Cleburne* (1985)

Cleburne,[1] decided a dozen years after *Moreno*, advanced the provocative, but undertheorized, analysis in *Moreno*. It considered the role of indirect bias—that is, the implications of legislators, not acting (as in *Moreno*) based on their own subjective dislike, but instead in response to such feelings expressed by their constituents. It also addressed, at least implicitly, what legislators' response to such biases means for the fate of more legitimate reasons offered in defense of the challenged discrimination. Finally, it examined these questions against a backdrop where the Court was presented with—and seems to have given at least some credence to—an argument that the group suffering from the challenged discrimination was one that merited heightened judicial protection across the board. For these reasons, *Cleburne* merits close attention.

Cleburne's Facts

In 1980, Jan Hannah purchased the house at 201 Featherston Street, in Cleburne, Texas, a town twenty-five miles south of Fort Worth. By that time Hannah had been working with intellectually disabled persons for over a decade. She intended the Featherston house to serve as a group home for thirteen mildly to moderately intellectually disabled persons,[2] under twenty-four-hour supervision.

The neighbors were not pleased. One of them was reported to have said, "The older women [in the neighborhood] are fearful of this thing. . . . [T]hey don't want these people around." The principal of Cleburne Junior High, located across the street, had different concerns: "Seventh- and eighth-grade kids may not always be the kindest people," he said. He continued, "It's a needed program. But the question is, is it needed at this site?" One neighbor seems to have summed up the attitude when he said. "We've lived here all our lives and we don't see why we should be subjected to this."[3]

The neighbors soon found allies. Cleburne's zoning ordinance allowed multi-person residences in the area encompassing the Featherston property; however, it excluded from that authorization "hospitals, sanitariums, nursing homes or homes . . . for the insane or feeble-minded or alcoholics or drug addicts" unless a special-use permit was obtained. In August 1980, the town zoning board denied Hannah's request for such a permit, and two months later the city council did so as well.

The zoning commission meeting was, according to press accounts, "stormy."[4] (And apparently of great interest to the community: The local newspaper carried accounts of that meeting and the subsequent city council meeting under banner headlines at the top of page 1.)[5] Almost a hundred persons attended the meeting.[6] Residents presented the zoning board with a petition opposing the home signed by twenty-nine residents. One resident stated, "I'm a coward. It's not a very pleasant thought to go to bed and know there's 13 demented, self-afflicted people across the street from you." When its own turn came to consider this issue, the city council, likely aware of the emotional debate before the zoning commission, limited public comment before voting 3–1 to deny the permit, citing concerns about traffic, overcrowding of the house, and the safe evacuation of the would-be residents given the home's location on a five-hundred-year floodplain. Reflecting on the controversy, the managing editor of the local newspaper (who wrote the articles covering the issue) concluded that the town had good reasons for denying the permit. However, he continued, "The rationale began forming after the emotional reactions."[7]

Of the three council members voting against the permit, one of them had served on the board of directors of a school for the intellectually disabled and one of them had an intellectually disabled grandchild. Regardless of any such personal sympathies, the city's decision still stung. As one of the would-be residents of the home remarked, "It hurts knowing the people in my hometown don't want me living there. It hurts real bad."[8]

The Opinion in *Cleburne*

In *Cleburne* the Court unanimously agreed that the city's actions violated the equal protection rights of the intellectually disabled. But it split badly on its reasoning. Writing for six Justices, Justice Byron White began by considering, and rejecting, the conclusion reached by the appellate court—that the intellectually disabled constituted a "quasi-suspect class" and thus merited heightened judicial scrutiny of its claims of unconstitutional discrimination. The Court's rejection of that conclusion meant that discrimination against the intellectually disabled received only rational basis review—as we have seen, the most deferential level of equal protection scrutiny. Nevertheless, the majority concluded that the city's decision failed even that low level of review. In particular, it concluded that the city's decision rested on "irrational prejudice" against that group. In making that determination, the Court appeared to rely heavily on the city's own argument that local residents had expressed to the city council their fear and apparent dislike of the would-be occupants of the group home.

The remaining three justices agreed with the Court's decision striking down the city's zoning decision. But that bloc, speaking through Justice Thurgood Marshall, argued that discrimination based on intellectual disability *should* be subject to heightened review, especially in cases, like *Cleburne*, that implicated important interests such as the right to establish a home.[9] But that was not the end of the justices' disagreement. Two justices in the majority concurred separately, to express doubt about the entire enterprise of courts differentiating their scrutiny of different types of discrimination.[10] Thus, the Court's core analysis—its determination that the intellectually disabled did not merit heightened scrutiny and its subsequent determination that the city's conduct nevertheless violated equal protection—was fully endorsed only by four Justices.

Why this fracturing? Part of the reason was the oddity of the Court's sequencing of its analysis—its rejection of heightened scrutiny for the intellectually disabled, followed by its conclusion that the city's action nevertheless failed lower-level, rational basis scrutiny. As Justice Marshall asked in his concurring opinion, why did the Court need to perform the first of those inquiries if it was going to find that, regardless of its outcome, the city failed to satisfy the default, rational basis, level of review? This result may well have been the result of happenstance: The justices' own records reveal that originally the Court was going to stop its analysis with the suspect class question and send the case back to the lower courts to apply the rational basis standard. Only later in their deliberations did the Court resolve to decide that latter question itself, but by that time at least a few of the justices had become entrenched in their approval of the Court's suspect class analysis and did not wish to excise it from the majority opinion.[11] But regardless of how the Court got there, the fact remains that it arrived at an odd place: first rejecting heightened scrutiny of the discrimination at issue, but then essentially deciding that that conclusion did not matter because the discrimination failed even a lower level of judicial scrutiny.

That latter result—the city losing under rational basis review—also raised its own questions. Such review is typically quite deferential—indeed, in addition to requiring only that the government action have a rational connection to a legitimate government interest, it also usually requires the plaintiff to *disprove* the existence of any such connection. That shifting of the burden of proof is usually fatal to plaintiffs raising equal protection claims. Yet in *Cleburne*, the Court applied a more stringent variety of rational basis review. It discounted the city's legitimate-sounding concerns about evacuating the group home during a flood; more generally, the Court noted the lack of any evidence in the record supporting a rational justification for the city's action. These two features of Justice White's opinions encapsulate the Court's deviation from standard-issue rational basis review: Under such review, essentially any legitimate-sounding justification will serve to validate the challenged discrimination, and the Court will not require actual evidence in the record proving that justification but, instead, will require the challenger to conclusively disprove it. In stark contrast, in *Cleburne* the Court did not accept that the city might have been motivated by the legitimate justifications it proffered,[12] insisting that such justifications be proven rather than merely hypothesized.

Cleburne's *Analysis*

These two oddities—the Court's decision to lead off with a suspect class analysis that Justice Marshall criticized as gratuitous, and its application of unusually searching review under the rational basis standard—provide us with an entry point for appreciating *Cleburne*'s contribution to the Court's evolving animus doctrine. Let's take them in opposite order, beginning with the Court's application of the rational basis standard. The Court began that application by noting the city's argument about local residents' fear of the intellectually disabled persons who would have occupied the group home. The Court pointed out that such negative attitudes would not have justified the residents in directly making the zoning decision themselves—for example, by referendum—and concluded that the city council's apparent acquiescence to those attitudes was similarly unconstitutional. Thus, the Court extended its analysis in *Moreno,* in which the Court suspected *legislative* animus, to a context in which it suspected legislative acquiescence to *constituent* animus.

In one sense this was not an extension at all. A year before *Cleburne* the Court had struck down the decision of a family law judge in a divorce case to award child custody based on social disapproval of the interracial marriage into which one of the divorcing parents had entered. In that case, *Palmore v. Sidoti,* the Court famously stated that "[p]rivate biases may be outside the reach of the law, but the law cannot, directly or indirectly, give them effect."[13] *Palmore,* however, dealt with private *racial* biases. *Cleburne,* by applying *Palmore* to a case of non-suspect discrimination, extended and generalized that prohibition.

But what about the decision that intellectual disability discrimination is non-suspect? Recall Justice Marshall's complaint that that determination was superfluous. On its face, his objection seems well founded: If the Court thought the city council's action violated rational basis review, why did it go through the effort of rejecting the plaintiffs' claim that intellectual disability discrimination merited more rigorous judicial review? As he put it, wasn't the Court's approach a case of "two for the price of one" decision making? While "two for the price of one" is a bargain at the supermarket, deciding two legal questions when only one is necessary to decide the case is not; indeed, the Court typically stresses that it decides only the questions necessary to resolve the case in front of it. So why did Justice White begin his opinion with a suspect class analysis that turned out to be superfluous?

As noted earlier, this sequencing may have derived from the evolution of the Court's decisional process—in particular, the desire of some justices to use *Cleburne* as a vehicle to limit the groups that enjoy suspect class status, regardless of whether the city's permit denial failed even rational basis review. But is there anything about the Court's suspect class analysis that may have influenced its seemingly distinct decision that the city's action failed rational basis review? Perhaps. Recall that Chapter 1 concluded with a brief explanation of the concept of a "suspect class." Suspect class analysis is an approach to equal protection that seeks to determine whether a particular species of classification—for example, on the basis of race, sex, or, as in *Cleburne*, intellectual disability—is so inherently problematic that courts are justified in being skeptical of (and thus scrutinizing carefully) every instance of such discrimination.

As Chapter 1 noted, this method of equal protection analysis arose from a famous footnote in an otherwise-insignificant case from 1938, *United States v. Carolene Products*,[14] in which the Court observed, among other things, that "prejudice against discrete and insular minorities may be a special condition, which tends seriously to curtail the operation of those political processes ordinarily to be relied upon to protect minorities, and which may call for a correspondingly more searching judicial inquiry." Eventually, the concepts in that phrase—"prejudice" "against discrete and insular minorities," and political process dysfunction—came to be encapsulated in a three-part test for determining whether discrimination against a particular group was suspect, thus justifying "more searching judicial inquiry." While expressed differently in different cases, for our purposes that test can be expressed as three inquiries: (1) Did the group in question suffer from a history of discrimination? (2) Is the trait that marks that group one that is immutable (that is, fundamentally unchangeable) and irrelevant to one's ability to contribute to society? and (3) Is the group politically powerless?

Suspect class analysis—what it is, how courts apply it, and whether it makes sense—is a far bigger topic than we can discuss here, in the discrete context of *Cleburne*'s application of that analysis. For our purposes, though, what is striking about *Cleburne*'s application is that at times it appeared to concede that the intellectually disabled satisfied at least some of the standard criteria. Not all of them, to be sure—the Court insisted that the intellectually disabled were "different . . . in relevant respects" from mainstream society and argued that society's provision of special education and other measures for their benefit "belies a continuing antipathy or prejudice" toward that group. Nevertheless, the Court's final justification for denying the intellectually disabled suspect class status appeared to concede that those persons did exhibit at least some indicia of a suspect class:

> Fourth, if the large and amorphous class of the mentally retarded were deemed quasi-suspect for the reasons given by the Court of Appeals, it would be difficult to find a principled way to distinguish a variety of other groups who have perhaps immutable disabilities setting them off from others, who cannot themselves mandate the desired legislative responses, and who can claim some degree of prejudice from at least part of the public at large. One need mention in this respect only the aging, the disabled, the mentally ill, and the infirm. We are reluctant to set out on that course, and we decline to do so.[15]

This quotation suggests that, in fact, the intellectually disabled may possess some of the traits marking a suspect class. Indeed, they may share such traits—"immutable disabilities," an inability to "mandate the desired legislative responses," and "some degree of prejudice from at least part of the public at large"—with many other groups. According to this last part of the Court's suspect class analysis, it is exactly the widely shared nature of those phenomena, and thus courts' inability to meaningfully explain why some groups experiencing these traits should be deemed suspect and others not, that justifies denying that status to the intellectually disabled. And it was only then that the Court started looking (unusually carefully, it turns out) for animus.

Connecting the Dots

But what is the connection? What does any of this have to do with animus? It is at least possible that the balance of the Court's analysis in *Cleburne*—in particular, its unusually careful scrutiny of the government's justifications for its actions—reflected its sense that *something* might be amiss with intellectual disability discrimination. Either the case for suspect class status was not fully made, or, as suggested by the quotation above, the case *was* made, but the Court was nervous about its ability to handle analogous claims that might be brought by other, similarly situated, groups. But either way, the case was at least partially made—that is, the intellectually disabled at least provided a partially convincing case that it was often the victim of unconstitutional discrimination.

If we understand the first part of the Court's opinion—the part where it considered, but rejected, suspect class status for the intellectually disabled—as sketching a picture in which that group was at least potentially at risk for unconstitutional discrimination, then the Court's unusually careful search for animus in the second part of its opinion becomes more comprehensible. On this understanding, the intellectually disabled convinced the Court that there was at least some reason to worry, at least some of the time, when that group was subject to disparate treatment. That argument may have simply fallen short, or, again as suggested by the paragraph quoted earlier, the Court may have simply concluded that courts could not competently apply heightened scrutiny in every situation in which the plaintiffs' analysis would have logically called for it.[16]

But if *wholesale* skeptical review of such classifications was inappropriate, then perhaps *retail*, or case-by-case, skepticism would be called for. But in which cases? *Cleburne* suggests two related answers. First, such skepticism is surely called for if, as in *Cleburne*, the government defendant "outs itself" by explicitly relying on private party dislike of the burdened group. Second, such skepticism may be appropriate if, again as in *Cleburne*, the background of the government's action lies within a constitutional "danger zone." In *Cleburne* itself, that danger zone existed because the victims of the government action—the intellectually disabled—appeared to have gone some way toward proving that they were a suspect class. To be sure, a court may not wish to accord heightened scrutiny to *every* decision falling within that danger zone—indeed, if it did, then it would simply declare the group a suspect class. But the proximity of a challenged decision to that danger zone might buttress the justification for heightened review when the particular context—here, the city's explicit embrace of the constituents' fear and dislike—independently justifies such careful scrutiny.

Cleburne's Significance

Cleburne adds two components to our understanding of animus. First, the city's reliance on private attitudes that, if expressed by the governmental decision maker itself, would have quickly and explicitly condemned its action, similarly condemned the city council's more indirect motivations. As the Court explained in both *Cleburne* and *Palmore* (the child custody/interracial marriage case from the year before), a governmental decision maker's reliance on private biases tars the challenged decision with those same biases. When such biases motivate government action, they become unconstitutional.[17]

Second, when discrimination falls on a group whose historical background suggests that it may frequently fall victim to unconstitutional discrimination, *Cleburne* implies that courts are justified in examining such discrimination more carefully. Normally, this heightened judicial review takes the form of suspect class status. But in a case like *Cleburne*, where the Court expressed concern about courts' ability to perform such review across the board to every case of intellectual disability discrimination, heightened judicial review may be reserved for special situations. *Cleburne* itself presented such a special situation because the city cited an unconstitutional motivation (constituent dislike of the group) for its decision. Of course, that justification is inadmissible, without any extra-careful scrutiny. But the city's reliance on that motivation perhaps justified more careful review even of the city's *legitimate* claimed justifications, such as its asserted flood evacuation concern.

Thus, perhaps Justice Marshall was too hasty when he accused the Court of gratuitously deciding the suspect class issue before striking the city's action down on rational basis grounds. Perhaps that previous decision was necessary to the latter one—not explicitly, but by creating the backdrop justifying more stringent review under the ostensibly deferential rational basis standard. On this theory, the Court's ultimate condemnation of the city's action as grounded in animus was aided, or prompted, by the groundwork it did earlier in the opinion—even if the Court did not take these steps fully consciously.[18]

Animus, then, might be more susceptible to judicial detection when a group has in fact suffered from discrimination in the past, when that discrimination is based on a factor that is immutable, and when that group continues to suffer from a lack of political power—even when a court is unwilling to connect those dots and explicitly deem that group a suspect class. Part II will connect those dots in a slightly different way. When it does, we will see that the emerging picture points in a surprising direction, but one that has close affinity to well-established equal protection law.

4

Romer and *Lawrence*

We must conclude that Amendment 2 classifies homosexuals not to further a proper legislative end but to
make them unequal to everyone else. This Colorado
cannot do.
—*Romer* (1996, Kennedy, J., majority opinion)

The Court has mistaken a *Kulturkampf* for a fit of
spite.
—*Romer* (1996, Scalia, J., dissenting)

Cleburne presented a situation in which the Court discerned in
the challenged law, not direct improper subjective motivation,
but responsiveness to such motives. Thus it can be understood
as a step removed from *Moreno*'s direct indictment of Congress's
motives. In the next case, *Romer v. Evans*,[1] the Court took a further step away from subjective motivations. *Romer* offers us a
glimpse into the Court's understanding of what animus means
when such subjective motivations are either not present or, at
least, when their identification presents difficult practical or conceptual challenges.

Amendment 2

After several municipalities in Colorado broadened their anti-
discrimination ordinances to include sexual orientation as a
protected status, a Colorado citizens group responded by placing on the November 1992 ballot a proposition, Amendment 2.

That proposition amended the Colorado constitution to prohibit "homosexual, lesbian or bisexual orientation, conduct, practices or relationships" from serving as the basis of a non-discrimination claim.[2] On election night, Colorado voters enacted Amendment 2 by a margin of 53 percent to 47 percent.[3]

The fight over Amendment 2 inspired strong feelings on both sides. Proponents argued that traditional moral values were imperiled by laws that banned discrimination against gays and lesbians. They insisted that they did not harbor dislike for gays and lesbians or intend to deprive them of equal rights. Instead, they described Amendment 2 as an attempt to ensure that gays and lesbians were not given "special rights." They acknowledged that such rights— that is, explicit inclusion in non-discrimination laws—might be necessary for other groups, for example, racial minorities. But Amendment 2's supporters insisted that gays and lesbians, who they described as an educated, affluent, and powerful political group, did not need such protections. Regardless of their sincerity, their "no special rights" slogan was effective. As one of the leaders of the anti–Amendment 2 campaign acknowledged, "In a microsecond they can say 'special rights' and send a message out. 'Gays don't deserve special rights.' And from our side it takes 10 or 15 minutes to undo that message. . . . So when you had 'special rights' versus something that takes 10 minutes to explain, who is going to win?"[4]

Beyond conceding the attractiveness of the message put out by Amendment 2's supporters, the provision's opponents—especially gay men and lesbians themselves—saw Amendment 2 in much more dire terms. Allegations of "hate" flowed freely, and after Amendment 2 triumphed at the polls it was common to hear of gays and lesbians expressing fear for their safety.[5] Looking back at that time, Angela Romero, a lesbian officer on the Denver police force, choked up, remembering her terror at the prospect of her career being ruined.[6] At least one gay Coloradan cited Amendment 2 in his suicide note.[7]

The Motives

Was Amendment 2 motivated by animus? Certainly its most prominent backers denied that. In an interview years later, a leader of the Amendment 2 campaign strongly resisted the charge that his effort was founded in dislike of gays and lesbians. Instead, he compared homosexuality to alcoholism, relating the story of a relative who was alcoholic and explaining that, while he loved his relative, that did not mean that he could approve of his alcoholism.[8]

Amendment 2's status as a voter initiative, rather than ordinary legislation, complicates any investigation into the enactors' subjective intent. After all, it is one thing to examine legislators' statements during a debate on a bill in order to determine their intent (as the *Moreno* Court did) but quite another to search for similar evidence of *voters'* intent. That is not to say that courts do not try. For example, they have attempted to discern the intent behind such initiatives by consulting the statements made in the official informational pamphlet sent to voters.[9] But this is nowhere near a perfect approach: Whatever a ballot pamphlet may say, voters may vote for a particular provision for all sorts of reasons.[10]

As an example, consider the material circulated by Amendment 2's supporters.[11] That material insisted several times that Amendment 2 would not deprive gays and lesbians of equal rights or intrude into their private sexual or lifestyle autonomy. But, as noted above, there is no guarantee that Coloradans voting for Amendment 2 shared those beliefs or expectations. Public opinion polls might help, but they are unreliable, given that poll results are known to vary depending on matters such as the way a question is framed.

But put those difficulties off to the side for now and consider those materials more carefully. They cast Amendment 2 as a denial, not of equal rights, but what they described as "special" rights—indeed, special rights of a pernicious type. In particular, they warned that without Amendment 2 it would become illegal for pastors to speak out against gays as a "deviant" group marked by what they believed to be immoral and destructive behavior, for schools to refuse to promote homosexuality as a desirable lifestyle, and for businesspersons and landlords to refuse to hire or rent to gays and lesbians based on the owner's or landlord's religious or moral views. Yet those materials insisted that Amendment 2 would not impact gays' and lesbians' equal rights in their capacities as "good employees minding their own business, etc."

Thus, according to these materials, if anyone's rights were being threatened by the status quo, it was the rights of Coloradans who disapproved of homosexuality, not the rights of gays and lesbians who were seeking inclusion in anti-discrimination laws.[12] Clashes of this sort are not uncommon in American law. The adage that "your right to swing your fist ends where my nose begins" reflects something real: Being forced to refrain from discriminating *does* implicate a would-be discriminator's rights to refuse to associate with members of particular groups—African Americans, Jews, or, in this case, gays and lesbians.

Ultimately, the question in such cases is, Whose rights should prevail? But for our purposes, we need to ask two (slightly) narrower questions. First, did Amendment 2 reflect a libertarian, "live-and-let-live" ethos, where everyone gets to live as they wish on equal terms but nobody is forced to bend their own beliefs to accommodate others? Or did it seek to oppress one group by leaving it defenseless against discrimination? Second, and more relevantly for us, how can we know which understanding motivated the 53 percent of Colorado voters who backed Amendment 2?

The example of the pro–Amendment 2 voter materials reveals the difficulty involved in answering this second question—and thus, by extension, the first question and, hence, the ultimate question about Amendment 2's constitutionality. Or at least it reveals the difficulty in answering this question by reference to the subjective intent of the body that enacted the law (here, the Colorado electorate). In most cases it is easy for proponents to offer legitimate-sounding reasons for a bill or initiative's burdening of a group. (Recall from the last chapter the city's flood evacuation argument in *Cleburne*.) In the case of Amendment 2, the argument appeared to be twofold. First, its defenders argued that gays and lesbians did not *need* protected status, as they were fundamentally different than other groups (such as racial minorities) that traditionally received such protection. Given that lack of need, the anti-discrimination rights Amendment 2 repealed constituted, in the pamphlet's repeated mantra, "special rights, not equal rights."

Second, those materials argued that such rights would cause other Coloradans affirmative harm by impairing citizens' speech, religious, and associational rights and by endorsing a lifestyle that, according to the proponents, was both voluntarily chosen and marked by conduct that was immoral and dangerous. As we will see in Part II, these arguments will bear on our construction of a theory of animus. But for now, note that the difficulty in concluding that such arguments reflect animus—and perhaps also the concern about explicitly accusing the people of Colorado of acting out of ill will—led the Supreme Court to take a different route to its animus conclusion.[13]

Amendment 2's Effect

Romer presented a number of issues relevant to equal protection analysis. First, the Colorado supreme court decided that Amendment 2 was unconstitutional for an equal protection–based reason completely distinct from our focus on animus. That court, relying on a line of Supreme Court cases stretching back to 1969, concluded that Amendment 2 violated gays' and lesbians' equal protection rights because it placed in the path of their political activity a hurdle that other groups did not confront: While other groups—say, women or veterans or the handicapped—could obtain anti-discrimination protection simply by winning victories in city halls across Colorado, after Amendment 2 gays and lesbians could obtain such protection only by successfully changing the state constitution, a much more difficult task.[14] We can safely ignore this issue—as interesting as it is—because the Supreme Court decided *Romer* on a largely different ground.

Second, Amendment 2 presented the thorny question, mentioned above, whether such anti-discrimination protection constituted "special rights" or simply "equal rights." The Court's decision on this question—the effect Amendment 2 had on the equal status of gays and lesbians in Colorado—was crucial to the Court's decision. After examining how the Colorado courts had construed Amendment 2, the Supreme Court concluded that the rights Amendment 2 denied to gays and lesbians were not mere "special rights." Instead, the Court described Amendment 2 as effecting a "[s]weeping and comprehensive" "change in [gays' and lesbians'] legal status." That change went beyond changes to traditional state anti-discrimination laws. Such laws—known as "public accommodations" statutes—historically required that a class of businesses including innkeepers and transportation companies (known as "public accommodations") be open to all who could pay. Over time, those laws expanded, both in terms of the businesses that were covered by the non-discrimination requirement and in the specification of certain classifications (most notably, race, but also including others) as forbidden grounds of discrimination. As the Court observed, Amendment 2 prohibited the inclusion of sexual orientation among those classifications.

But Amendment 2 did much more. As the Court noted, it also prohibited Colorado officials from including sexual orientation among the protected classifications with regard to *governmental* discrimination—for example, in government employment or at state universities. Indeed, one of the plaintiffs in the case was Angela Romero, the lesbian police officer in Denver mentioned earlier. Romero was identified buying a book at a lesbian bookstore, after which she was demoted and transferred.[15] Ultimately, she assisted in developing a department-wide policy prohibiting discrimination against gay and lesbian officers—a policy that Amendment 2 threatened to undo, at the possible cost of her career.[16]

Finally, the Court suggested that Amendment 2 might even go beyond prohibitions on non-discrimination rules focusing specifically on gays and lesbians to include prohibitions on any claim that a gay man or lesbian might make that a state entity engaged in arbitrary discrimination by denying him or her service or protection because of sexual orientation. Early in the oral argument at the Court, Justice O'Connor pushed the state's attorney on the question whether Amendment 2 would allow a public library in Colorado to deny borrowing privileges to a person because of her sexual orientation.[17] As trivial as this example sounds, it stands for something quite important. As the Court observed in *Romer*, a fundamental requirement of American law prohibits government from acting arbitrarily—for example, a city library denying a library card to a lesbian for no good reason, regardless of whether the library had a policy banning sexual orientation discrimination. Ultimately, the Court's opinion in *Romer* picked up on Justice O'Connor's concern: Amendment 2, the Court implied, might indeed allow such arbitrary discrimination when it was perpetrated because of the victim's sexual orientation.[18]

The Court's Decision in *Romer*

Thus described, Amendment 2 constituted, in the Court's view, an unusual law that "confounds" traditional equal protection scrutiny. Recall from earlier chapters that such traditional scrutiny—so-called rational basis scrutiny—seeks to determine whether the challenged classification has a rational relationship to a legitimate government interest. As we saw in *Moreno* and *Cleburne*, that review is normally quite deferential: Unless the challenged classification is one that the Court has identified as particularly pernicious, or "suspect," courts will normally grant the legislature great leeway when reviewing it. Thus in most cases courts uphold government classifications even when they have a less-than-perfect fit with the asserted government interest.

According to the Court, Amendment 2 "confounds" that inquiry because of its "across the board"[19] denial of protection to a group identified by a single trait (that is, their sexual orientation). The Court viewed such a blanket denial—that is, a classification that applies across all spheres of social life and government action—as a literal violation of the guarantee that all persons enjoy the equal protection of the laws. According to the Court, Amendment 2 essentially (and unconstitutionally) told gays and lesbians, "We have our laws, for the protection of all—except for you." As Justice Kennedy phrased it at the end of his opinion, "We must conclude that Amendment 2 classifies homosexuals not to further a proper legislative end but to make them unequal to everyone else. This Colorado cannot do. A State cannot so deem a class of persons a stranger to its laws."[20]

The Court then moved on to a second inquiry, one it described "conventional and venerable" and "related" to the first one: whether Amendment 2 satisfied the rational basis test. Colorado argued that Amendment 2 served two legitimate government purposes: protecting other citizens' freedom of association (in particular, the rights of Colorado landlords who objected to renting to gays and lesbians), and conserving the state's anti-discrimination enforcement resources to combat what the state perceived as more serious forms of discrimination.

The Court did not question the legitimacy of these interests—thus the state satisfied the first component of standard equal protection scrutiny, that a law be justified by a legitimate, public-regarding interest. However, it concluded that Amendment 2 failed the second part of that requirement: that there be a reasonable fit between those interests and the law's classifications. As you might imagine, Amendment 2's "fit" problem arose because the interests Colorado cited did not require the law's across-the-board prohibition on non-discrimination legislation. Quite simply, local laws preventing the Denver Police Department, the Aspen Public Library, or the Boulder Hilton from discriminating against a lesbian had nothing whatsoever to do with the associational rights of a homeowner who refused to rent his spare bedroom to one. Given that poor fit, the Court found that Amendment 2 failed that "conventional and venerable" requirement.[21]

Here's where animus came in. The Court's conclusion that Amendment 2 failed the rational basis test raised, in the Court's mind, "the inevitable inference that the disadvantage imposed [was] born of animosity toward the class of persons affected." In other words, if Amendment 2's breadth meant that the legitimate justifications Colorado offered were simply not credible, then something else must have been afoot. With nowhere else to look, the Court concluded that that "something else" was animus.

Understanding *Romer*

Uniting the Analysis

On one understanding, *Romer* tells a straightforward story. All legislative classifications must be justified by a legitimate interest, to which the classification must have a reasonable degree of fit. Amendment 2 simply did not fit with any legitimate interest Colorado offered. But since every law must have a justification, the lack of any legitimate justification must mean that it was motivated by an illegitimate one. QED.

But we can say something more than this, something that unites the two strands of the Court's analysis. Recall the first strand: the Court's concern, seemingly distinct from any fit requirement, about Amendment 2's breadth. Amendment 2 did not discriminate against gays and lesbians with regard to a particular subject matter—for example, marriage, eligibility for a tax exemption, or service in a police department. Instead, it classified across the board: According to the Court, Amendment 2 quite possibly meant that no person could complain about any discrimination of any sort that was founded on his or her sexual orientation.

The Court wondered: What could this law possibly be getting at? To the Court, it seemed that Amendment 2 simply sought to classify against gays and lesbians *because they were gays and lesbians*. Not because, for example, same-sex unions did not further the purposes of marriage, not because gay men did not need a particular tax exemption, and not because service as a police officer was inconsistent with lesbian identity. There was, literally, no referent for the discrimination Amendment 2 authorized. The only thing that mattered, it seemed, was that the discrimination be based on sexual orientation.

So understood, we can start to see how the two pieces of *Romer's* analysis fit together and, in turn, how those two components suggested the presence of animus. The breadth of Amendment 2's discrimination made it impossible to examine the law for a reasonable relationship to a legitimate government interest—the boundlessness of its discrimination simply "confound[ed]" any evaluation of the law's fit to such an interest. To be sure, Colorado offered up two such interests (other citizens' associational freedom and the conservation of the state's enforcement resources). But when the Court got past its original exclamation at the law's raw breadth and moved on to its "second and related point," it found that Amendment 2's discrimination "outr[a]n and belie[d]" those facially legitimate justifications.

In other words, Amendment 2's breadth—the first strand of its analysis—set up the Court's conclusion that it failed the conventional equal protection requirement of "fit"—the second strand. And, to repeat, once it concluded that that "fit" requirement was not satisfied, it looked around for a justification that *might* fit Amendment 2's breadth. All that was left standing was animus. And indeed, as an explanation, animus fit Amendment 2 pretty well. Since all Amendment 2 referred to was a type of discrimination (that is, since it did not specify a particular social context in which that discrimination would be allowed), the only explanation for it was that Coloradans wanted gays and lesbians to be unequal as a general matter.

The Dissent

Justice Scalia, joined by Chief Justice Rehnquist and Justice Thomas, would have upheld Amendment 2. Scalia disputed the Court's suggestions about Amendment 2's breadth, agreeing with the provision's sponsors that it merely prevented gays and lesbians from enjoying specially protected status in Colorado law. But even the remaining breadth did not concern him because he thought that Coloradans had *the right* to express disapproval of homosexuality by denying sexual orientation any protected status in Colorado law. For Justice Scalia, Amendment 2 reflected one position in a cultural debate—hence, his reference, quoted at the start of this chapter, to a Kulturkampf.[22] In his view, the fact that the Court had in 1986 upheld a law criminalizing homosexual *conduct*[23] necessarily meant that a state could take the "anti" side in the cultural debate about *homosexuality* and homosexual *persons*. One can certainly debate that point—although it became moot in 2003 when the Court overruled that 1986 precedent.[24] But on its own terms, what it meant for Justice Scalia is that an anti-gay "cultural struggle," or Kulturkampf, could not, by definition, reflect unconstitutional animus.[25]

Amendment 2 and the Meaning of Animus

What does this analysis tell us about animus? Begin where we started this chapter. Unlike in *Moreno* and *Cleburne*, the Court in *Romer* did not suggest that it actually found direct evidence of animus. Instead, the Court found animus as "an inevitable inference." The Court's phraseology makes a great deal of sense once one considers the process by which Amendment 2 was enacted. Amendment 2 was a voter-approved initiative, rather than a statute enacted by the state legislature through the normal law-making process. That distinction matters. While, as in *Moreno*, it might be possible for a court to comb through the legislative history to uncover Congress's subjective motivations, and while, as in *Cleburne*, it might be possible to conclude that the city council responded to its constituents' subjective motivations, it is much harder to directly condemn voters' motivations as subjectively ill willed. Indeed, trying to identify a single purpose motivating a voter-enacted initiative, and then testing that purpose to ensure that it is focused on the public good, presents not just practical problems but also theoretical ones.

Practicalities

As a practical matter, while it may be credible to claim to have discovered the motivations of a legislature of a hundred or so representatives, it is far harder to do the same when the relevant "legislature" consists of millions of voters. Undoubtedly some Coloradans voted for Amendment 2 because they simply disliked gays and lesbians. But others likely voted for it for other reasons: Some may have disfavored anti-discrimination laws of any sort; others may have been neutral on the underlying question but simply believed that Colorado municipalities should not have their own anti-discrimination policies. As judges in recent cases have concluded when evaluating challenges to anti-same-sex marriage initiatives, it is simply impossible to know what might have motivated voters supporting such measures. Indeed, judges have agreed on this point even while disagreeing on the larger point about such measures' constitutionality.[26]

In a different, but similarly practical vein, it might simply be impolitic for a court to accuse the citizens of a given jurisdiction of animus. One legal scholar, discussing the Supreme Court's 2013 conclusion that the federal Defense of Marriage Act (DOMA) was motivated by animus, criticized the Court's approach as a "jurisprudence of denigration."[27] Indeed, dissenting in *Romer*, Justice Scalia accused the majority of "insulting" the people of Colorado when it *inferred* animus. Imagine the "insult" if the Court had been more explicit!

Democratic versus Republican Lawmaking

But an even more fundamental problem exists with divining, and then passing judgment on, voter intent. As naïve as this may sound, our system is based on an expectation that legislators will decide to vote for or against bills based on their conception of the public good. Consider, for example, a speech made by the famous English political theorist Edmund Burke, responding to the argument that a member of Parliament should be bound to vote in ways instructed by his constituents:

> Parliament is not a congress of ambassadors from different and hostile interests; which interests each must maintain, as an agent and advocate, against other agents and advocates; but [rather] parliament is a deliberative assembly of one nation, with one interest, that of the whole; where, not local purposes, not local prejudices, ought to guide, but the general good, resulting from the general reason of the whole.[28]

But such high-minded deliberation aimed at "one interest, that of the whole," is not necessarily demanded of individual voters. Union members or business owners may vote—either for particular initiatives or for representatives—based on what they promise to deliver for unions or businesses. To be sure, union members and business owners, channeling the famous (but slightly misquoted) statement of the head of General Motors, may believe that "what's good for unions/businesses is good for the nation."

And, indeed, one theory of politics holds that, even once the legislature is elected, the lawmaking process is one in which different groups, each promoting their own interest, meet and bargain and hammer out compromises based on each group's relative political strength.

Still, with the legislative process we might expect such bargaining to take on at least the patina of regard for the public good; at the very least, we might indulge in the fiction that legislators vote based on their conception of the greater public good. Recall Edmund Burke's statement, quoted above: The job of a legislator, he argues, is not simply to serve as a transmission belt for his constituents' preferences but, instead, to deliberate with his colleagues and seek to vindicate, "not local purposes" motivated by "local prejudices," but "the general good, motivated by the general reason of the whole." Such deliberation, at least ostensibly aimed at furthering the public good, is at least arguably not even a theoretical requirement of lawmaking through voter initiative. Indeed, in a real way, the difference between the obligations of these two lawmaking bodies (the legislature and the people as a whole) demarcates the difference between, respectively, a republican form of government and a pure democracy.[29]

This is not to say that voters deciding on initiatives should feel free to vote their private prejudices when acting as lawmakers— that is, when voting "yes" or "no" on initiatives. Even less is it to say that the citizen-enacted status of a law immunizes (or should immunize) it from judicial scrutiny. Recall that *Cleburne* stated quite plainly that unconstitutional laws enacted by legislatures do not suddenly become constitutional when enacted via voter referenda.[30] But it does suggest that the problem with identifying animus in Amendment 2 goes beyond the practical problem of entering into the heart and mind of every Colorado voter who pulled the "yes" lever. Instead, this understanding of the difference between voter initiatives and legislatively enacted statutes suggests that animus simply may not be a coherent concept—or perhaps may be a less coherent concept—when one considers voter-enacted legislation such as Amendment 2.

This insight may help explain why the *Romer* Court did not directly accuse the people of Colorado of acting out of animus. To be sure, the accusation *was* leveled—but only indirectly, as the only possible explanation for Amendment 2 after more legitimate justifications for the law had been tested and found insufficient. Indeed, it was leveled only after the Court concluded that Amendment 2 was unconstitutional for failing to satisfy traditional rational basis review.

But regardless of what it was based on—a lack of meaningful evidence, politeness, or a more theoretical concern for what voters can legitimately do when they act as lawmakers—the fact remains that in *Romer* the Court found animus indirectly, as an inference to be drawn from objective factors such as the challenged statute's unusual breadth. This is appropriate: Such factors *should* matter to the animus inquiry, and not just when the challenged law takes the form of a voter-enacted initiative. Even if we acknowledge that it may be less troubling for courts to insist that *legislators* act in pursuit of the public interest, we still encounter serious concerns about the credibility and appropriateness of judicial decisions striking down laws based on a legislature's presumed subjective bad intent. Thus, even though *Romer*'s more indirect animus conclusion may have rested in part on the character of Amendment 2 as a voter initiative, as we will see its analysis is useful more generally, when courts consider animus allegations leveled at a legislature's enactment.

As we will see in Part II when we unite Part I's insights into a theory of constitutional animus, *Romer*'s concern about the breadth of a challenged law reflects an important indicator that animus may be afoot. But, *Romer* implicitly acknowledged, such an indicator is just that—a symptom, or warning sign, of the underling constitutional violation. As merely a warning sign of a violation, such breadth does not condemn the law. But it does justify a closer judicial look—just like the one the Court took in *Romer* itself.

Lawrence v. Texas and Justice O'Connor

This chapter concludes with a brief discussion of the next case to discuss animus, *Lawrence v. Texas*.[31] Unlike the other modern animus cases, *Lawrence* does not get its own chapter because, for our purposes, its importance lies mainly in the concurring opinion of Justice O'Connor, rather than in the statements of the Court itself. *Lawrence* involved a challenge brought by two gay men, John Geddes Lawrence and Tyron Gardner, to their arrest and conviction for violating Texas's sodomy law.[32] When the case got to the Court, six justices voted to strike down the Texas law. Five of them, speaking through Justice Anthony Kennedy (who also wrote the opinion in *Romer*), held that the Texas law violated the men's right to liberty under the Fourteenth Amendment's Due Process Clause. In doing so they overruled a case from 1986, *Bowers v. Hardwick*, which rejected a similar due process challenge to Georgia's sodomy law.

Justice O'Connor was the sixth vote to strike the Texas law down. But she had joined the *Bowers* majority seventeen years earlier and declined to join Justice Kennedy's opinion resting on the Due Process Clause and overruling *Bowers*. Instead, she argued that the Texas law, which criminalized only same-sex sodomy, violated Lawrence's and Garner's equal protection rights. In so arguing, Justice O'Connor invoked the animus concept the Court had introduced in *Moreno* and had applied in *Cleburne* and *Romer*. Explaining that concept, she wrote:

> Laws such as economic or tax legislation that are scrutinized under rational basis review normally pass constitutional muster, since "the Constitution presumes that even improvident decisions will eventually be rectified by the democratic processes." *Cleburne v.*

Cleburne Living Center. We have consistently held, however, that some objectives, such as "a bare . . . desire to harm a politically unpopular group," are not legitimate state interests. *Moreno.* See also *Cleburne*; *Romer.* When a law exhibits such a desire to harm a politically unpopular group, we have applied a more searching form of rational basis review to strike down such laws under the Equal Protection Clause.[33]

Applying these principles, Justice O'Connor explained that Texas's invocation of morality as a justification for banning same-sex, but not opposite-sex, sodomy constituted moral disapproval of a *group*, rather than moral disapproval of *conduct*, which *Bowers* had validated as a legitimate state interest. By contrast, she said, again citing *Moreno* and *Romer*, "Moral disapproval of [gays and lesbians], like a bare desire to harm the group, is an interest that is insufficient to satisfy rational basis review under the Equal Protection Clause."

Justice O'Connor's concurrence is important for two reasons. First, her suggestion, in the last sentence of the paragraph quoted above, that a finding of animus triggers heightened review, raises a thorny conceptual issue for our understanding of animus: Can a law infected by animus nevertheless be upheld, if it survives that heightened review? Chapter 8 will discuss that issue; here we can only flag it. Second, her reliance on *Moreno*'s animus idea reinforced that idea's power in modern Supreme Court jurisprudence. It suggested that justices would be open to claims of animus in cases that went beyond situations like *Moreno* and *Cleburne*—in which explicit dislike appeared to be motivating the challenged discrimination—and beyond situations like *Romer*—in which the law imposed such a broad disability that it was impossible to credit any legitimate justifications. This validation, and possible expansion, of the animus idea opened the door to the Court using animus doctrine as a tool in a larger variety of cases. The next chapter considers the most recent case in which the Court made use of that tool.

5

United States v. Windsor

DOMA seeks to injure the very class New York seeks
to protect.
—*Windsor* (2013)

United States v. Windsor[1] is, as of this writing, the last of the cases
firmly and explicitly grounded on an animus theory. (The 2015
decision striking down state same-sex marriage bans, discussed
in Chapter 12, is more equivocal on this point.) In many ways it is
also the most paradoxical. It seemed to matter greatly to the Court
that the statutory provision *Windsor* struck down, Section 3 of the
Defense of Marriage Act (DOMA),[2] had the effect of disrespecting
states' decisions about who could marry whom, yet it disclaimed
reliance on federalism. Its focus on that disrespect would seem to
buttress, not limit, states' autonomy to provide or deny marriage
rights to same-sex couples, yet after the opinion came down a long
string of federal judges cited it when striking down state same-sex
marriage bans.

Perhaps most relevant for our current purposes, at one level the
Court's animus conclusion seems straightforward (if nevertheless
highly controversial): In finding animus, the Court relied heavily on
actual statements of Congress's purpose and even the statute's title.
But on the other hand, its animus conclusion appears to result from a
complex interaction of factors, some of them (most notably, the statute's disrespect of state marital decisions) not even directly related to
equal protection at all. Given these puzzles—and especially in light
of *Windsor*'s impact on same-sex marriage claims beyond the limited
confines of federal recognition—it bears giving this case a close look.

Windsor's Facts

Windsor is an utterly dry case about the amount of estate tax a surviving spouse owes the federal government. But—of course—it is much more than that. As the stories introducing the prior three chapters have made clear, abstract (though important) legal issues often come wrapped in deeply human personal stories. The story of *Windsor* is no less human for being straightforward: Edie Windsor and Thea Spyer loved each other for over forty years, and when they had an opportunity to get married they did. *Windsor* was the culmination of Edie's challenge to the federal government's refusal to accept New York's recognition of their marriage.

That refusal was not the first instance of discrimination Edie Windsor faced. At work, she never came out as lesbian during the sixteen years she worked for IBM, even to her co-workers, whom she called "my buddies."[3] In an act of passing that any gay or lesbian person of a certain age (and many younger ones) would recognize, when in 1967 Thea proposed to Edie she gave Edie a diamond pin, rather than a ring—a ring would have raised too many questions.

Of course, Edie's and Thea's engagement in 1967 could not have led to a marriage that any government would have recognized—no governmental authority in the world recognized same-sex marriage until the Netherlands, in 2001.[4] After 2001, a trickle of foreign nations and American states began to recognize same-sex marriage unions. The supreme court of Edie and Thea's home state, New York, decided in 2006 that the state constitution did not guarantee same-sex marriage rights. However, in 2008, New York, though a combination of legislative and gubernatorial action, recognized same-sex marriages legally performed elsewhere.

By then, Edie and Thea had married, in Canada. By 2007 Thea had suffered a number of health setbacks; in that year her doctor warned her she had less than a year to live. Wishing to die married to the woman she loved, Thea—confined to a wheelchair owing to multiple sclerosis—and Edie traveled to Toronto, where they were married by Canada's first openly gay judge. Friends had to lift Thea's hand up so she could receive her wedding ring. She died in 2009.

In 2009, a federal law, the Defense of Marriage Act, had been on the books for thirteen years. The Defense of Marriage Act was Congress's reaction to early marriage rights litigation, which bore preliminary fruit in the mid-1990s. The prospect of one state potentially recognizing same-sex marriage had galvanized anti-marriage-equality forces that feared that such legalization would open the door to more widespread recognition. One part of DOMA responded directly to that fear by preventing federal courts from insisting that a state recognize a same-sex marriage validly performed in another state. Another part of DOMA, Section 3, provided that, for federal law purposes, marriage consisted only of a union between one man and one woman.

One of those federal laws was the Internal Revenue Code. When Thea died, the IRS, citing Section 3, disallowed the estate tax exemption Edie would otherwise have enjoyed by virtue of New York's recognition of her Canadian marriage. That discrimination prompted Edie to sue.

Windsor's Analysis

As noted in the introduction to this chapter, *Windsor*'s analysis of DOMA is at once straightforward but also layered and complex. The Court, speaking again through Justice Kennedy (who has written the Court's four opinions vindicating gay rights claims), began by acknowledging both the normal practice of states enjoying primary authority for defining marriage and the eligibility for marriage, as well as the federal government's power, when managing its own programs, to override state choices. But despite that latter power, he noticed something unusual about DOMA. In particular, he noted its broad reach, affecting, as he wrote, "over

1,000 federal statutes and the whole realm of federal regulations." Importantly, the Court then immediately reminded the reader: "And [DOMA's] operation is directed to a class of persons that the laws of New York, and of 11 other States, have sought to protect." Even at this early stage of its analysis, then, the Court was painting a picture of an unusual law—unusual in its deviation from the normal federal practice of respecting state marriage decisions and in its "reach and extent," not just to "over 1,000 federal laws," but also to a particular class to whom (by 2013) eleven states had decided to make available the dignified status of "married." Citing his own opinion in *Romer*, Justice Kennedy then reminded readers that "discriminations of an unusual character especially suggest careful consideration to determine whether they are obnoxious" to the Constitution.[5]

In the next section of his opinion, where he considered the implications of all this, he pulled no punches. "DOMA," he said, in the very first sentence of that section, "seeks to injure the very class New York seeks to protect." Immediately moving to *Moreno*'s statement that, "at the very least . . . a bare congressional desire to harm a politically unpopular group cannot" justify disparate treatment of that group, Justice Kennedy then choreographed an intricate dance between federalism, equality, and fundamental rights: "The responsibility of the States for the regulation of domestic relations is an important indicator of the substantial societal impact the State's classifications have in the daily lives and customs of its people." Based on that observation he concluded that "DOMA's unusual deviation from the usual tradition of recognizing and accepting state definitions of marriage here operates to deprive same-sex couples of the benefits and responsibilities that come with the federal recognition of their marriages. This is strong evidence of a law having the purpose and effect of disapproval of that class."

At this point Justice Kennedy then moved on to the direct evidence of congressional intent—speeches and statements on the floor of Congress and the title of the statute. But before getting there, let us pause to inspect the stage Justice Kennedy had set against which to evaluate that evidence. Up to this point in the opinion, he has described DOMA as a law that deviates from the normal federal practice of respecting state law marriage definitions and does so in a way that is both across-the-board (the "over 1,000 federal statutes" it affected) and narrow (focusing solely on same-sex marriage). Moreover, DOMA imposed this unusual, both-broad-and-targeted disability in an area carrying significant dignitary interests—the area of marital rights.

So understood, Justice Kennedy's description of DOMA shared important features with Amendment 2, the Colorado initiative the Court struck down in the *Romer* opinion he authored seventeen years earlier. Just like Amendment 2, DOMA denied a targeted group (again gays and lesbians) rights across the board. And just like he had in *Romer*, Justice Kennedy in *Windsor* cautioned that such an unusual law merited closer judicial scrutiny. But his description of DOMA suggested that there was even more cause for concern. In Justice Kennedy's view, DOMA denied a uniquely meaningful right—the right not to have one's lawful marital status denied by the federal government. Moreover, the fact that marital status was granted by states and then denied by the federal government rendered DOMA, if not a violation of federalism (something Justice Kennedy disclaimed), then at least another reason to be suspicious.

All of these warning signs set the stage for Justice Kennedy's examination of DOMA's text and legislative history. That examination "demonstrate[d] that interference with the equal dignity of same-sex marriages, a dignity conferred by the States in the exercise of their sovereign power, was more than an incidental effect of the federal statute. It was its essence." As if to reinforce the interlocking nature of his federalism, substantive rights, and equality arguments, he concluded, after quoting from the bill's supporters and the title of the bill itself, that "[t]he arguments put forward by [DOMA's congressional supporters at the Court] are just as candid about the congressional purpose to influence or interfere with state sovereign choices about who may be married." The intimately connected nature of those arguments is reflected in his observation that, while New York, in granting same-sex marriage rights, "sought to eliminate inequality," DOMA "frustrates that objective" by "writ[ing] inequality into the entire United States Code."

Let us cut through the detail and think about the structure of this argument. After painting a picture of DOMA as even more suspect than Amendment 2, Justice Kennedy, armed with that suspicion, then found his worst fears confirmed by the text of the statute and the rhetoric of its sponsors. In other words, those earlier observations about DOMA's unusual nature gave Justice Kennedy cause to look carefully for animus. And when he did, he found it.

This analysis makes it more understandable why Justice Kennedy did not emphasize the normal step of considering whether DOMA was rationally connected to any legitimate government purpose. Don't forget that he took care to note that step in *Romer*, concluding that Amendment 2 failed the rational relationship test given the extremely bad fit between the state's justifications and the classification Amendment 2 created. He downplayed that inquiry in *Windsor*, a fact Justice Scalia noted in his dissent. But understanding the structure of Justice Kennedy's opinion reveals why that de-emphasis makes sense if one has a particular understanding of animus. If one believes that animus is an affirmative constitutional violation—that is, if a conclusion that a statute is motivated by animus is fatal to the statute's constitutionality, regardless of its other merits—then it makes sense for a judge to strike a law down as soon as he concludes that animus is in fact the reason behind a statute. No search for a redeeming justification is necessary. Game over.

And this is what Justice Kennedy did—almost. After reciting both DOMA's text and the rhetoric of its supporters, he then returned to the effect DOMA had on state-recognized same-sex marriages. That recitation led him to conclude that DOMA's effect was to place such marriages at a second-class level—literally, as valid for state law purposes but not federal law ones. Then, in the penultimate substantive sentence of the opinion, he finally mentioned, if only by implication, the rational basis requirement:

> The federal statute is invalid, *for no legitimate purpose overcomes* the purpose and effect to disparage and to injure those whom the State, by its marriage laws, sought to protect in personhood and dignity.[6]

So it turns out there *was* a conclusion about the rational relationship test. Unfortunately for all of us, Justice Kennedy did not explain the process by which he performed that test. Indeed, he did not even *identify* the legitimate purposes DOMA might be thought to serve—a point Justice Scalia made in his dissent, which *did* identify some potential legitimate purposes behind DOMA.

The point here is not that Justice Scalia had the better of the argument with regard to the rational relationship test. It is, instead, to acknowledge that even Justice Kennedy implied that he had performed rational relationship review, even after concluding that DOMA was motivated by a "principal purpose . . . to impose inequality."[7]

Did he need to make this concession at the very end of his opinion? Was there anything gained by at least nodding in the direction of traditional rational relationship review? Indeed, did he add that last phrase simply in response to Justice Scalia's dissent (which would have been circulated before the opinions were finalized)? While we will likely not know the answer to this final question until justices' papers from this case become available, at least we can think about the first two. Viewed one way, his acknowledgment of rational relationship review, even if conclusory and perhaps even an afterthought, nevertheless brought his opinion within the channel cut by the earlier animus opinions, including his own opinion in *Romer*. All of those earlier opinions—*Moreno*,

Cleburne, and *Romer* (as well as Justice O'Connor's separate opinion in *Lawrence*)—considered whether the challenged action promoted a legitimate government interest. Thanks to his quick rejection of DOMA's rational basis, so did *Windsor*. In fact, Justice Kennedy's very brief application of traditional rational basis review placed *Windsor* not just within the channel cut by the earlier animus cases but also within the much broader channel of equal protection review more generally.

That brief nod in the direction of traditional rational basis review may also have reflected Justice Kennedy's desire to avoid confronting an interesting, important, but difficult problem—indeed, a problem on which Part II of this book will focus. By concluding, however quickly, that DOMA did not serve any legitimate government interest (or at least any such interest that "overcame" its disparaging purpose and effect), Justice Kennedy was able to avoid asking the following question: To what extent and by what mechanism does a legitimate motive cleanse a law of the taint of animus?

The Defense of Marriage Act itself provides an illustrative example of this question. In *Windsor*, Justice Scalia protested that DOMA did in fact survive rational basis scrutiny because it arguably promoted legitimate government interests (which is all that scrutiny requires). For example, he argued that DOMA avoided enmeshing the federal government in the difficult question of which state's laws to apply to a same-sex couple for federal income tax purposes when a couple married in marriage equality jurisdiction A and then moved to marriage inequality jurisdiction B.[8] Accept for the moment Justice Scalia's argument that DOMA did in fact rationally further this government interest. What would that conclusion mean? Would it mean that DOMA was not really motivated by animus because it featured this second, more benign, set of effects? Or would it mean that DOMA might still be motivated by animus but that its promotion of a legitimate government interest served to cleanse (or, to use Justice Kennedy's language, "overcome") that illegitimate motivation?

It may seem like a hair-splitting distinction to ask whether Justice Scalia's argument, if accepted, rescued DOMA from the allegation of animus or whether that rational justification stood alongside the animus conclusion but sufficed to provide the necessary justification needed for the statute to survive rational basis review. But this distinction is important. It is important as a practical matter because, depending on the approach we take, we may ask different questions, or at least apply different standards when answering them. It is also important theoretically. If we adopt the first of these views (that a benign explanation for the statute cleanses it from the stigma of animus), we can still conclude that statutes without such a cleansing—statutes that we do in fact label as based in animus—are unconstitutional, full stop. But if we adopt the other approach, then we sign up for the proposition that a statute may be labeled as reflecting "animus" but nevertheless may be constitutional.

Again, Justice Kennedy's cursory rejection of any such rational basis allowed him to avoid these questions. But as observers attempting to make sense of the doctrinal concept of animus, we do not have the luxury of forcing the facts into conceptually simple packages. *Windsor*, as the last case to date to explicitly rely on the animus idea, leaves us with the question of how to relate allegations of unconstitutional animus to responses that, in fact, the challenged law promotes legitimate government interests and hence is constitutional. In a sense, it forces us to return to the question with which we started this book: What exactly counts as unconstitutional animus, and how do we uncover it? The cases we have examined in Part I provide us with the tools we need to construct a doctrinal structure answering that question. But those cases have not built that structure. That task will fall to us in Part II.

* * *

Part I of this book has identified, explained, and discussed the major modern Supreme Court statements about animus. Those statements have made clear that animus is a real concern of the Court. Nevertheless, that doctrine remains undertheorized. For example, these cases do not explicitly explain how animus can be identified. *Moreno* appeared to indict the subjective motivations of the congresspersons who reveled in the chance to deny food stamps to "hippies," and *Cleburne* rejected as illegitimate the city council's seeming capitulation to constituent dislike of the people they wished to exclude from the neighborhood. But in *Romer*, Justice Kennedy notably declined to directly accuse the people of Colorado from acting out of ill will. How necessary is such subjective ill will to a conclusion about animus?

Consider some of the other factors the Court focused on in these cases. In *Romer* Justice Kennedy emphasized the breadth of the burdens Amendment 2 imposed on gays and lesbians. Similarly, in *Windsor* he noted DOMA's applicability to "over 1,000" federal statutes. In both of these cases he characterized the challenged laws as unusual. While these considerations make intuitive sense as warning signs about a law's fundamental fairness and thus its constitutionality, intuitions by themselves are insufficient. Can we find a doctrinal foundation for these and other commonsense warning signs?

Finally, what result does an animus conclusion yield? One might think that, of all these questions, this one is the easiest: Given how troubling "animus" is as a motivation for government action, one might think that surely, once we find it, that should be the end of the case. But remember what Justice O'Connor said in *Lawrence*, describing the Court's animus cases up to that point: "When a law exhibits such a desire to harm a politically unpopular group, we have applied a more searching form of rational basis review to strike down such laws under the Equal Protection Clause." While the last part of that sentence ("to strike down such laws") jibes with our intuition, we have to pay attention to the first part of the sentence ("When a law exhibits such a desire . . . we have applied a more searching form of rational basis review"). Is animus really a magic weapon—what one scholar describes as a silver bullet[9]—that is necessarily fatal to a statute? Or is Justice O'Connor telling us that animus merely triggers "a more searching form of rational basis review"? And what about the very last phrase, which states that that "more searching . . . review" triggers a strike-down? Giving Justice O'Connor credit for accurately describing the Court's animus jurisprudence, it appears as though we need to investigate more carefully the consequences of a court uncovering animus.

The cases I have described in Part I raise these, and other, questions. They constitute the raw materials and tools constituting the Court's animus doctrine. But the lack of clear answers to important questions those cases pose means that the Court has not yet used those materials to construct a coherent structure. That's what Part II sets out to do.

PART II

Building the Structure

6

What's Wrong with Subjective Dislike?

The concept of an intent for . . . an institution is
hilarious.
—Judge Frank Easterbrook (1992)

The title of this chapter is a play on words. Of course, there is a
lot wrong with "subjective dislike." Even Justice Scalia, who would
have upheld Colorado's Amendment 2 and the federal Defense of
Marriage Act despite the majority's conclusions that those laws
were based in animus, recognized in *Romer* (the Amendment 2
case) that "it is our moral heritage that one should not hate any
human being or class of human beings." But the point of this chapter is not to repeat that well-accepted moral argument. Instead, it
is to investigate what else is "wrong" with subjective dislike—in
particular, what's wrong with a doctrinal theory that requires
investigation whether the challenged law is, in fact, grounded on a
subjective dislike of the group that law burdens. It turns out there
is something wrong with that approach.

From Subjective to Objective

The Supreme Court has already traveled this same ground, albeit in
a slightly different context—the interpretation of a Reconstruction-
era statute, the Ku Klux Klan Act of 1871. As you might guess from
its informal title, that statute focuses on private persons attempting
to deprive other persons of their constitutional rights, including
equal protection. The statute provides victims with a right to sue
when "two or more persons . . . conspire or go in disguise on the

highway or on the premises of another, for the purpose of depriving . . . any person or class of persons of the equal protection of the laws or of equal privileges and immunities under the laws."[1]

Interpreting that language in *Griffin v. Breckenridge*, a seminal 1971 case, the Court said that "[t]he language requiring intent to deprive of equal protection, or equal privileges and immunities, means that there must be some racial, or perhaps otherwise class-based, invidiously discriminatory animus behind the conspirators' action."[2] It was easy for the Court to find animus in *Griffin*—or at least to find that the plaintiff, an African American in Mississippi in 1966, had pleaded animus. He had alleged that the defendants had mistaken him for a civil rights worker and had captured and beat him in order to deprive him of the equal enjoyment of a variety of federal rights, such as the right to free speech and interstate travel. In the context of the time, place, and circumstances, it was undeniable that the defendants' alleged conduct, if proven, reflected animus of the most malicious sort, however we define that concept.

Twenty-two years later, the Court faced a harder case arising under that same law: anti-abortion protesters who had violently blocked access to an abortion clinic.[3] The clinic had alleged (among other things) that the protesters were motivated by animus against women. The Court rejected that argument. For our purposes, the reasons for that rejection are less important than how the Court understood the (statutory) animus requirement:

> We do not think that the "animus" requirement can be met only by maliciously motivated, as opposed to assertedly benign (though objectively invidious), discrimination against women. It does demand, however, at least a purpose that focuses upon women *by reason of their sex*—for example (to use an illustration of assertedly benign discrimination), the purpose of "saving" women *because they are women* from a combative, aggressive profession such as the practice of law.[4]

These two cases cover a great deal of ground in our consideration of animus. To be sure, they do so in interpreting statutory, not constitutional, language. And indeed, that statutory language did not itself include the word "animus"—the two cases interpret that word as itself an interpretation of the statutory language.

Nevertheless, the Court's progression—from finding it obvious that violently expressed racial discrimination constitutes animus to noting, two decades later, that "maliciously motivated . . . discrimination" is not a requirement for animus—is instructive for our examination of animus as a constitutional law issue. First, in both situations the Court was in the position of understanding the legal text (the Klan Act and the Equal Protection Clause) as including an inquiry into animus. Thus, in both cases animus was not itself the textual legal rule but an interpretation of it, which in turn required additional interpretation. Second, both of those legal texts speak to the same wrong—the deprivation of "the equal protection of the laws." And, indeed, as we will see, the Court's progression in these two cases—from applying animus in the most obvious, undeniable form to thinking about its application in more nuanced cases—tracks our own. I don't have the space here to delve into the possible reasons the Court recognized that, for purposes of the Klan Act, animus could include what it called "objectively invidious" intent (as distinguished from intent that is "maliciously motivated"). But it is striking that there, as in our constitutional context, the Court recognized that "animus" could be found via such "objective" intent—whatever that concept might mean in a given context.[5]

Subjective Dislike: The Obvious Issues

To say that the Court has recognized that animus may be objectively discernable and not just subjective is not to deny the force of subjective dislike. On the contrary, understanding animus as subjective dislike is utterly intuitive. If animus is "bad," then naturally we think of "bad actors." Justice Scalia himself constructed the template for such villains: To use his words from his dissent in *Romer*, quoted above, anyone who "hate[s] any human being or class of human beings" is betraying "our moral heritage." Surely that must be what "animus" means.

But problems immediately bubble up from this starting point. Begin with the most basic problem: Legislatures are not human. That is to say, legislatures, as corporate bodies composed of multiple human beings, do not have a collective conscience—or a collective will. In a fundamental way, a legislature cannot "hate." Of course, we speak all the time about "legislative intent." But when we scratch a little deeper, we find that such references sometimes point to statements of intent made by particular legislators—for example, sponsors or supporters of a bill—rather than the legislators' own collective intent. Such statements may be persuasive evidence of what a court concludes the statute means. Recall that in *Moreno*, the Court determined the intention behind Congress's enactment of the revised food stamp "household" definition by referring to a committee report and a legislator's statement made during floor debate on the bill.

But such references cannot be understood as reflecting the legislature's subjective intent. After all, legislatures are multi-member bodies; different members may have very different subjective intentions when voting for (or against) a bill. Without proof that a sponsor's or a supporter's or even a committee's statements were adopted by enough legislators to constitute a majority (or whatever proportion is required to enact the bill into law), we cannot say that such statements by themselves reflect the subjective intent of "the legislature." A prominent federal judge and scholar once stated that "the concept of an intent for . . . an institution is hilarious."[6] One does not have to go that far in order to agree that such a concept is, at the very least, problematic.

Before we accept that verdict and move on, however, we need to stop and recognize one limitation to this otherwise commonsense critique of subjective bad intent. Sometimes equal protection claims do not arise out of impersonal, institutional conduct. Instead, they sometimes arise out of individual conduct shorn of any institutional process. Consider an extreme example of this phenomenon: the "class of one." This strange little doctrine, which a federal judge once called "a murky corner of equal protection law,"[7] involves claims of discrimination based not on group membership (for example, race or sex discrimination) but, rather, simple claims that a government official has treated similarly situated persons differently—not based, say, on their race or their sex but, instead, as a "class of one." Such claims often feature allegations that the government—almost always an individual government official, rather than, say, a legislature—has a grudge against the plaintiff. As one might imagine, such claims involve colorful facts: a town official who insisted that one particular homeowner give the city, in response for town utility service, an easement greater than other landowners had been required to give[8] or, in one particularly egregious case, a group of policemen who conspired to ticket their enemy's car so frequently that he was able to show that the tickets purported to show the car in two different parts of Chicago at the exact same time.[9]

Beyond being fun to read, class-of-one cases illustrate two important points. First, the nature of the particular government action at issue matters when we consider the usefulness of the concept of subjective intent. Such subjective ill will may be a more difficult concept to accept when we are talking about legislative action, but it may make much more sense when we are talking about the personal spats that form the core of class-of-one cases.[10] Second, as distant as class-of-one cases are from equal protection's core concern with group-based discrimination, the realization that animus in its most explicit form may play an important role in those cases suggests that animus is an appropriate part of the equal protection inquiry more generally, even if it is harder to uncover in the context of institutional decisions. Combining these two insights helps us realize both that animus is relevant to equal protection law but that that concept may mean different things in different contexts.

One of those contexts is institutional action: a statute, a regulation, or a governmental institution's collective policy or decision. As we have seen above, in that context the critique of subjective ill will is well founded. Of course, one might still attempt to infer intent from objective indicators—that is, one can still approach statutory interpretation fundamentally as a matter of uncovering legislative intent, even if one abandons a search for any subjective will on the part of "the legislature." Indeed, it is common for courts to employ such indicators to discern a legislature's intent. For example, a judge might attempt to determine the legislature's intent in enacting a particular statute by considering which interpretation best harmonizes all of the statute's provisions into a coherent unit. The theory here is that the legislature is presumed to have intended to enact a coherent statute; thus, the interpretation that accomplishes that end would be understood as the meaning the legislature intended and hence the correct interpretation.

But this theory is controversial. Most important, it assumes that the legislature did in fact intend to create a harmonious statute. Other explanations of the legislature's action are certainly possible. For example, one might just as easily conclude that the statute was a collection of compromises that resulted in a less-than-fully consistent total package. Assuming that the legislature did in fact have a single purpose in mind thus constitutes a value choice on the part of a court—a choice to impose on statutes an internal coherence they may lack. But other objective tools are also available to courts seeking to discern a legislature's "intent" in the particular context of discrimination. Indeed, the next chapter will offer a set of such tools.

Subjective Intent and Citizen Governance: Voters and Jurors

Stop for a moment, and consider how far afield this analysis has taken us with respect to animus. Recall that the question this chapter addresses is whether subjective dislike is the best way of approaching the question of animus. There is no real way to decide that a statute is in fact thus motivated unless one is willing to examine the subjective motivations of the legislature. On one understanding, dislike is visceral: Speaking about it as the logical conclusion from an analysis of objective factors drains the concept of so much of its force as nearly to redefine it. If one is going to accuse a person—or a legislature—of acting out of dislike, then one might well be committed to basing that conclusion on an estimation of the subjective motivations of the actor. As suggested above, that is a difficult task when applied to a legislature.

It is even more difficult when one considers voter initiatives, such as Colorado's Amendment 2. Unlike, say, the members of the Colorado legislature, the voters of Colorado did not have to explain themselves when they stepped into the voting booth. (To be sure, legislators are under no legal obligation to do so either, but we intuitively expect legislators at least to be willing to explain their votes when asked. In fact, on many issues legislators are enthusiastic about doing just that.)[11] Indeed, unlike a legislature, which at least has an apparatus by which its members can explain themselves—committee reports, floor speeches, and the like—the voters of a given jurisdiction have no ready-made mechanism by which they can officially register their views.

As I noted in Chapter 4 when discussing Colorado's Amendment 2, courts faced with constitutional challenges to voter-enacted provisions have resorted to creative, if indirect, ways of divining voters' intent. For example, they have scrutinized the ballot materials circulated by the group supporting the enacted provision.[12] But, as that chapter concluded, any conclusions that could be drawn from that sort of inquiry are necessarily indirect and, hence, less reliable. They are especially unreliable when the question sought to be answered is the subjective motivation of hundreds of thousands of voters.

To illustrate this, recall what I said in my discussion of Amendment 2. The pro-Amendment side's materials insisted that that side did not wish to deny gays and lesbians of equal rights—they stated again and again that their opposition was to what they called gays' demands for "special rights" and, indeed, the rights deprivations *others* would suffer if non-discrimination laws prevented anti-gay Coloradans from refusing to hire or rent to gays. Presumably, some Coloradans voted for Amendment 2 for these reasons. But just as presumably, especially given the heated cultural wars of the 1990s, others favored it exactly because they thought it would deprive gays of rights. Indeed, the modern phenomenon of "dog whistle" politics—in which advocates for a particular candidate or a position refrain from making explicit particular arguments pro or con but instead use symbols or coded terminology to make their points—strongly suggests that simple reliance on the actual words used by those advocates cannot be understood as complete and infallible guides to what the voters must have intended—an intent that voters were under no obligation to disclose.

A distant echo of these problems arose in 1987 when the Court considered whether Georgia's capital punishment scheme was unconstitutional because it was racially biased. Warren McCleskey, a death row inmate, argued that it was statistically far more likely that a convicted murder defendant would receive the death penalty if the defendant himself was black or the victim was white. He received the assistance of a statistician who provided the results of sophisticated statistical analysis demonstrating that those two variables—the race of the defendant and the race of the victim— played critical roles in determining when Georgia juries recommended death sentences.

The Supreme Court, however, was unwilling to conclude that those statistics demonstrated the requisite intent to discriminate on the basis of race. For our purposes, what is most notable about the Court's analysis was its observation about the role of juries in our system. Writing for the five justices in the majority, Justice Powell noted that juries are not required to explain their decisions, including their decisions about recommending a particular sentence. Indeed, not only were they not required, "controlling considerations of . . . public policy dictate[d] that jurors cannot be called . . . to testify to the motives and influences that led to their verdict."[13] Without the ability to hear the explanation for a particular jury recommendation, the Court was not willing to conclude that the aggregate of jury recommendations across all capital cases in Georgia reflected discriminatory intent in McCleskey's particular case. Regardless of what one thinks about the ultimate conclusion in that case, the analogy between one type of citizen exercise of sovereign power (the initiative process) and another type (the criminal sentencing process) suggests the difficulty of uncovering intent in either case.

Summing Up: The Limitations of Subjective Intent

My tentative conclusion from all this—that it may be difficult to expect a credible answer to the question whether a particular law was motivated by its enactors' subjective dislike—presents problems for animus doctrine. Our most intuitive understanding of animus is that it reflects exactly what this analysis suggests is difficult to uncover: subjective dislike. This reality requires that we shift our focus away from that idea and construct a new understanding of animus, one that focuses on an understanding that is more accessible to discovery by courts.

To be sure, understanding animus as a subjective mind-set remains useful, at least to the extent that it reflects our intuitions of what "animus" really means. That understanding can serve as a reference point, allowing us to evaluate any more objective theory by measuring the extent to which a more objective theory resonates with our intuitional understanding. Nevertheless, to the extent the epistemic difficulty of uncovering that subjective intent pushes us away from making that the focal point of our inquiry, we need to refocus our analysis toward a more "constructed" intent—that is, an intent that is more amenable to discovery in the real world of judicial review of legislative action. Thus, the way forward lies in deciding what objective evidence is relevant to that "constructed" intent and what that evidence tells us. When we decide that, the best, most judicially accessible, understanding of animus should appear.

The next chapter takes up this work.

Objectively Objectionable

Determining whether invidious discriminatory
purpose was a motivating factor demands a sensitive
inquiry into such circumstantial and direct evidence
of intent as may be available.
— *Village of Arlington Heights v. Metropolitan Housing
Development Corp.* (1977)

Chapter 6 explained why our first, most intuitive, cut at identifying animus fails to provide a workable judicial approach. The
proof problems that arise when we seek to determine whether a
challenged law exhibits the lawmakers' subjective dislike of the
burdened group requires that we consider another approach, one
that is grounded in objective factors. This chapter considers that
approach and what it suggests for our ultimate understanding of
the concept of unconstitutional animus.

Constitutional Equality/Constitutional Intent

The alternative approach we will be thinking about remains based
in notions of illegitimate government intent. As such, it helps to
consider how the Supreme Court has thought about such intent in
analogous circumstances. The most logical place to begin that process is with *Washington v. Davis,*[1] the 1976 case in which the Court
held that alleged discrimination of a certain type—for example, on
the basis of race—would be treated as such only if the government
either facially classified on that basis or enacted a formally neutral
law that nevertheless evinced an intent to classify on that ground.

The first of these possibilities—a facial classification on the ground alleged to violate the Constitution—is one we can dismiss for our purposes, as there is no easy analogy to a law that facially reflects animus. Instead, it is the second of these possibilities that matters to us. This second situation envisages a situation in which a legislature has classified in a facially neutral way—for example, by instituting a race-neutral requirement before someone can get a government job—but did so with an intent to exclude persons based on a particular characteristic—in this example, race.

Just to be clear—and to make a point that I will make continually over the course of the remaining chapters—discriminatory intent is not the same as unconstitutional animus. "Discriminatory intent" sounds bad—maybe just as bad as "animus." But, just like "discrimination" itself, discriminatory intent does not itself amount to a constitutional violation. Instead, "discriminatory intent" refers to an intent to classify on a particular ground, such as race. A conclusion that such intent exists triggers whatever judicial scrutiny the Court has determined is appropriate for that type of discrimination—for example, "strict scrutiny" for race, and "intermediate scrutiny" for sex. Such scrutiny is not necessarily fatal; in 2003, for example, the Court upheld the University of Michigan Law School's use of race in its admissions policy. For our purposes, the basic point is simple, if not necessarily intuitive: A finding of discriminatory intent is not the same as a finding of unconstitutional discrimination, as similar as they sound. This chapter establishes the basic building blocks of discriminatory intent and explains how those tools help us understand animus. The next chapter explains why the two concepts, while related, are not identical.

The Building Blocks of the Intent Requirement

As noted above, the Court formally established the intent requirement in the 1976 *Davis* case. *Davis* dealt with a Washington, D.C., requirement that candidates for the police academy attain a particular score on a test. The test itself was race neutral: There was nothing in it that mandated a higher or lower score for a given candidate based on the candidate's race. But the test did have a disparate racial impact: Blacks failed the test at a higher rate than whites.

In *Davis* the Court held that this "mere" disparate impact did not reflect discriminatory intent. Thus it did not make out a case of race discrimination that would in turn be subject to the heightened scrutiny that such intentional discrimination triggers. At the same time, the Court made clear that discriminatory intent does not require a conclusion about the government decision maker's subjective mind-set.[2] Instead, objective considerations may inform a court's inquiry into whether such intent exists. For example, in *Davis* itself, the Court explained that the bare, objective fact that a law's burdens fall more heavily on one group than on another might suffice to demonstrate discriminatory intent, if that disparate impact is unexplainable on any other ground.

This principle had surfaced, at least implicitly, earlier in the Court's jurisprudence. One example is a 1960 case, *Gomillion v. Lightfoot*.[3] *Gomillion* involved the decision by the Alabama legislature to redraw the boundaries of the City of Tuskegee, converting its shape, in the Court's words, "from a square to an uncouth twenty-eight sided figure." Beyond the aesthetic unpleasantness of the resulting shape, this switch had the effect of removing all but "four or five" of the city's four hundred African American voters, without removing a single white voter.[4] The Court had no difficulty concluding that such objective facts, if proven at trial, made out a violation of the Fifteenth Amendment's guarantee against racial discrimination in voting.

There is good reason to consider the impact of a law as an important indicator of its intent. Justice Stevens, who always had doubts about the meaningfulness of the difference between intent and impact, explained that one of the best indicators of what the legislature intended to do was what it in fact accomplished—that is, the impact of its work. This is particularly the case given the inherent difficulties, discussed in Chapter 6, of uncovering the subjective intentions of a multi-member body such as a legislature or city council (not to mention the voters of an entire jurisdiction). When the search for intent thus shifts to second-order, indirect considerations, the impact of the challenged action is often as good a factor as can be found of what the legislature intended to accomplish. Indeed, our search for the legislature's intent would be assisted by inquiring, not just into the impact itself, but whether that impact was understood to be inevitable and thus was foreseeable.[5]

The Court has identified other factors as well. One year after *Davis*, the Court set forth a number of indicators, beyond the extent of the law's disparate impact, that were relevant to the discriminatory intent question. In *Village of Arlington Heights v. Metropolitan Housing Development Corporation* (1977),[6] the Court considered a racial discrimination challenge to a town's denial of a zoning variance to a builder who wanted to build multi-family housing that was expected to be racially integrated. The town's decision did not explicitly invoke race: Nowhere did the town officially announce that the integrated character of the housing development prompted the denial. In deciding whether that decision nevertheless reflected racially discriminatory intent, the Court explained that "the historical background of the [challenged] decision," "the specific sequence of events leading up to" it, "departures from the normal procedural sequence," "substantive departures," and "the legislative or administrative history" of the decision were all relevant considerations.[7] Let's consider these factors in more detail.

The Historical Background

A complaint often leveled at law is that it is formalistic—that is, that it is blind to the underlying realities of a given situation. This is sometimes expressed via the famous statement of Anatole France about the majestic equality of law, which forbade both rich and poor from sleeping under bridges, begging in the streets, and stealing bread.[8] But law, at least at its best, *is* aware of social realities. For example, in *Griffin v. County School Board of Prince Edward County* (1964), the Court considered a challenge to a Virginia county's refusal to desegregate its schools. In rejecting the argument that federal courts should refrain from deciding the case until state courts had had a chance to consider it, the Supreme Court cast away barren formalisms about state-federal relations— important, to be sure—in light of the historical background of the fight to desegregate schools in the Commonwealth:

> It is argued that the [federal] District Court should have abstained from passing on the issues raised here in order to await a determination by the Supreme Court of Appeals of Virginia as to whether the conduct complained of violated the constitution or laws of Virginia. . . . But we agree with the dissenting judge in the Court of Appeals that this is not a case for abstention. . . . [We] hold that the issues here imperatively call for decision now. The case has been delayed since 1951 by resistance at the state and county level, by legislation, and by lawsuits. The original plaintiffs have doubtless all passed high school age. There has been entirely too much deliberation and not enough speed in enforcing the constitutional rights which we held in *Brown v. Board of Education* had been denied Prince Edward County Negro children. We accordingly reverse the Court of Appeals' judgment remanding the case to the District Court for abstention, and we proceed to the merits.[9]

The historical background mattered to the *Griffin* Court. That background convinced the Court that this was not an everyday case in which concern for federal-state relations counseled federal courts' staying their hand until state courts had had a chance to resolve the relevant state law issues. So too, historical background would matter to a court considering a claim that a challenged law was motivated by discriminatory intent. If, for example, a given jurisdiction had had a history of discriminating against the relevant group—just like Prince Edward County had had a history of obstructing school desegregation—then otherwise neutral justifications for a result, such as a federalism-based argument for federal judicial abstention, would have to give way in light of what was really going on. In *Griffin*, what was really going on was an ongoing, persistent attempt to use any means possible to frustrate school desegregation. In the context of discriminatory intent, if what is really going on is long-standing historical disfavoring of a particular group, then the facial neutrality of a law should not conclusively prove the lack of discriminatory intent.

The Specific Sequence of Events

Sometimes the appropriate analytic lens is more focused than such long-standing history. In other words, sometimes the appropriate historical investigation of the state's challenged action should focus, not on the overall history of the decision maker's conduct, but on its actions with regard to the specific challenged action.

Reitman v. Mulkey (1967)[10] is a difficult case and thus presents an illuminating example of this factor. *Reitman* involved California's Proposition 14, a voter initiative that successfully sought to repeal fair housing legislation the California legislature had enacted over the previous several years. At issue in *Reitman* was whether Proposition 14, by repealing that legislation—and, crucially for the Court, inserting into the California constitution a right on the part of private landowners to discriminate—involved the state sufficiently in such private discrimination as to make the state itself guilty of discrimination in violation of the Fourteenth Amendment.

Reitman is not a case about discriminatory intent per se; indeed, it was decided a decade before *Washington v. Davis* established the intent requirement. But *Reitman* considered an equally vexing and similarly contextual question, known as the "state action" question: When does a state's approval of private discrimination so involve the state in that discrimination as to make it fair to attribute that private discrimination to the state and thus trigger the Fourteenth Amendment? (Recall that the Fourteenth Amendment prohibits *states*, not *private parties*, from depriving persons of equal protection.) In answering that question, *Reitman* considered, among other interpretive aids, what it called "the facts and circumstances concerning the passage and potential impact of [Proposition 14], and . . . the milieu in which that provision would operate." In other words, it considered, to use *Arlington Heights'* terminology, "the specific sequence of events leading up to" the challenged action.

This inquiry was made necessary because of a very basic fact about California and every American jurisdiction: There is no federal constitutional requirement that any state or city prohibit private discrimination. To be sure, today most states do—most states at least have "public accommodations" laws that prohibit certain types of discrimination in the provision of goods and services such as transportation and amusement. But there is no constitutional requirement that they do. From this it follows—and the dissenters in *Reitman* stressed—that California was under no constitutional obligation to retain the anti-discrimination legislation that was the target of Proposition 14. In other words, California, if it wished, never had to enact such legislation. Similarly, it could choose to repeal it at any time.

But isn't that what Proposition 14 did? Not exactly, according to the *Reitman* majority. That majority agreed with the state court that Proposition 14 involved the state closely enough with private discrimination as to transmute that private action into "state action" that violated the Fourteenth Amendment. The Court reached this conclusion after reviewing the analysis of the California court. In turn, the state court had based its decision in part on the wording of Proposition 14, which did not simply repeal the earlier nondiscrimination legislation but inserted into the state constitution "the right of any person . . . to decline to sell, lease or rent [his real] property to such person or persons as he, in his absolute discretion, chooses." But the Court also noted the California court's conclusion, based on the sequence of relevant events, that "the ultimate impact of [Proposition 14] in the California environment" was to "encourage and significantly involve the state in private racial discrimination contrary to the Fourteenth Amendment."

As our introduction to this subsection conceded, *Reitman* is a tough case. But what is relevant for our purposes is how *Reitman* implicitly applied the principle that the "sequence of events leading up to" the challenged action can be relevant to a determination of discriminatory intent. As with the other *Arlington Heights* factors, this factor is solidly grounded in common sense: In making a determination about discriminatory intent, of course we would want to know the history of the issue in question—not just the long-ago history (as the first *Arlington Heights* factor suggests) but the "specific sequence of events" that precipitated the challenged action.

Reitman illustrates this idea, in the similarly fact-intensive and contextual area of determining when a state is so closely associated with private conduct as to be constitutionally responsible for it. In the abstract, it might be perfectly appropriate for a state to repeal an anti-discrimination statute and even less objectionable (at least constitutionally) to refrain from enacting one to begin with. Similarly, it might be perfectly acceptable for a legislature to enact a law that simply happens to have a disparate impact on the basis of some constitutionally problematic ground, such as race or sex—at the very least, current constitutional doctrine is not troubled by a law merely because it has such disparate impact. But if the events leading up to that enactment (what the *Reitman* Court called the background "environment") suggest something more sinister—in *Reitman* itself, a desire to applaud or encourage private discrimination, and in the discriminatory intent context, an intention to actually impose the disparate impact the law imposes—then we would have a different situation. And that is what this particular *Arlington Heights* factor calls for: an investigation into whether such bad intent can be uncovered in that sequence of events. As we will see, this very commonsense idea will play an important role when we consider how we should analyze allegations of animus.

Procedural Departures

Sometimes the best indicator of a decision's legitimacy is how normally or abnormally it was reached. A decision that is rushed through, exempted from normal deliberative procedures, or shunted away from the normal decision maker naturally raises suspicions that something nefarious is going on. The value of procedural regularity goes beyond the efficiency and predictability that comes along with such regularity—the value, that is, of procedure for its own sake. In addition, by subjecting similar issues to similar decisional processes, governments (and other institutions) help ensure substantively fair treatment. Indeed, it also helps ensure that such decisions are *perceived* as substantively fair. To drive this point home, consider a simple thought experiment. If all criminal defendants were tried according to the same procedure, but then one particular defendant was tried according to a different process, we would immediately wonder whether that latter defendant was being singled out for a substantively different result. It might be more lenient or it might be harsher. But we would suspect that something (substantive) was up.

The *Arlington Heights* Court applied this factor.[11] It noted that the zoning decision at issue had not been rushed through or shunted into a closed-door meeting. Indeed, Justice Powell observed that the town had provided additional meetings in order to provide for a full ventilation of views. To be sure, from the opinions of the Supreme Court and the lower court one senses that much of that ventilation consisted of neighboring homeowners' opposition to the project. There is thus at least the possibility that the town's procedural care added fuel to the fire of opposition— opposition that, as we will see later, appeared at least partially race based. Ironically, then, if the town's decision was suspect because of the procedure it employed to make it, it was because it provided *too much* procedure. But this irony simply reinforces the basic point: The regularity of a procedure—its consistency with procedures used to decide analogous questions—should militate in favor of finding nothing substantively amiss.

Substantive Departures

As the previous subsection explained, one of the major benefits of procedural regularity is that it helps ensure substantive regularity. Such substantive regularity is, of course, crucially important when considering whether something invidious is lurking in governmental action. If procedural irregularity is two steps removed from a core conclusion about the invidiousness of a facially innocent government action, then substantive irregularity is only one step removed. To return to our earlier example: We might be concerned if a criminal defendant was singled out for a trial process to which no other defendant was subjected. But we would be even more concerned if he was subject to a different law than every other defendant who engaged in the same conduct.

Again, *Arlington Heights* itself is a good illustration of both the importance of this criterion and also its limitations. Recall that that case considered a town's denial of a zoning change request made by a non-profit real estate developer that wished to build low- and moderate-income multi-family housing on land that was zoned for single-family homes. When the Court got to the factor we are now focusing on—whether the challenged decision reflected a substantive departure from previous actions—the Court observed that the town had been "committed" to single-family residences "as its dominant residential land use." More specifically, it noted that the land surrounding the proposed development was all zoned for single-family use and recognized that landowners adjoining the parcel likely purchased their land in reliance on the entire area being committed to single-family housing. Finally, the Court took notice of the town's policy to zone land for apartment buildings in "buffer" areas between single-family neighborhoods and commercial or manufacturing districts. The proposed rezoning of the plaintiff's parcel for apartment use would have conflicted with that long-standing town policy.

The picture painted by the Court was thus of a zoning policy that was in place long before the plaintiff's housing project entered the picture. The town's rejection of the rezoning request was consistent with that policy—in particular, the town's "commitment" to single-family residences and its limitation of multi-family housing to "buffer" areas. Indeed, in recognizing the reliance interests of the neighboring landowners on the continued single-family character of the neighborhood, the Court took substantive consistency to an even higher level. That recognition elevated the role of such consistency beyond simply tending to disprove discriminatory intent, instead making it a positive justification for the law—that is, as a protection for those reliance interests. Given this picture, then, the town's denial of the zoning change request represents nothing to be concerned about.

But still, there are limits to the usefulness of this factor. Why? Because things change. In particular, conditions change such that the justification for a particular government action can shift, or take on new content or significance, even when the challenged action can be accurately described as substantively consistent with what came before it.

To see this, return again to *Arlington Heights*. The Court in that case determined that the town's zoning change denial was substantively consistent with its past attitudes toward multi-family housing. To speak very approximately, the town "passed" the substantive consistency "test." But the Court also noted that the area where the town was located had historically been home to very few racial minorities. Thus, it is quite possible that the challenged zoning decision was the first one that had direct implications for its racial composition. In a real way, then, there was no *relevant* prior practice to which the challenged decision could be compared for consistency.

Consider how we might apply this idea to contemporary controversies. Hypothesize a state that for a century or more had defined marriage as consisting of one man and one woman. Such a law might have originally been viewed as neutral toward sexual orientation, even though today we would understand such a law as aiming at gays and lesbians who might wish to wed. Indeed, before the "invention" of the idea of homosexual persons in the late nineteenth century, a claim that an opposite sex-specific marriage law discriminated against gays and lesbians might have been met with uncomprehending stares.[12] Rather than as an act of discrimination against gay persons, such a law could have been enacted either as a housekeeping measure, simply to make clear, legally, who could get married, or perhaps as focusing on plural marriages, which were a highly controversial issue in the later part of the nineteenth century, when Utah and other western territories with heavy Mormon populations sought admission to the Union. Could a state argue that there was nothing out of the ordinary in its denial of a marriage license to a same-sex couple because such a denial was substantively consistent with its long-standing practice—indeed, with its practice back to a time when same-sex marriage was not an issue and discrimination against homosexuality not even comprehensible because homosexuality as a category had not yet been invented?

If this example seems far-fetched, return to *Arlington Heights* itself. If racial exclusion had never driven the city's zoning decisions, perhaps because racial minorities had never sought to live there, then what is the real significance of the fact that the city's zoning decision—when racial exclusion *was* an issue[13]—was consistent with those previous decisions? Certainly, one cannot indict the decision as intentionally based on race just because it did something that happened to have a racially disparate impact (unless that disparate impact was so overwhelming that the decision was, to use the Court's words, "unexplainable on grounds other than race").

My point, instead, is more limited but still important: If race had never been an issue in the town's zoning decisions, then the town's alleged race-based denial of that request should not be exonerated simply because the town had always zoned in this way before. That consistency certainly does not hurt the town's defense. But whether it *helps*—and, if so, by how much—remains uncertain. If this analysis is correct, then perhaps this *Arlington Heights* factor, as intuitively sensible as all the others, is not as probative as one might have originally thought.

Legislative/Administrative History

The final *Arlington Heights* factor inquires into the relevant decision makers' specific intent when enacting the challenged law—most notably, by considering the statements those officials made in connection with their decision. There is an obvious logic to such an inquiry when one is seeking to uncover the intent behind a government action. That logic is highlighted when one contextualizes this factor with the other *Arlington Heights* factors. The second of those factors—the historical background of the decision—addresses the intent question most generally, by asking about the deep history of the particular issue. The third factor, by investigating the specific sequence of events leading up to the challenged law, focuses the court's attention more narrowly on the particular challenged law. This final factor, by considering the evidence of the relevant decision makers' specific intent when enacting the challenged law, is the most focused of all.[14]

Taken together, this history—at its broadest, then more focused, and finally most specific—can be understood as counseling a holistic examination of what we can intuitively understand as the government's "intent." The other three *Arlington Heights* factors—the extent (and foreseeability) of the disparate impact, and the procedural and substantive regularity of the challenged decision—add an objective gloss to that inquiry. They complement the factors discussed in the prior paragraph by providing objective reasons to worry that that history did in fact suggest bad intent.

Thus, just like the other *Arlington Heights* factors, an investigation into the legislative or administrative history of a challenged decision makes good common sense, as one input among several in reaching a holistic conclusion about intent. Still, challenges await any investigation into legislative history. Consider *Arlington Heights* itself. The Court noted the trial court's observation that "some of the opponents of Lincoln Green [the contested housing project] who spoke at the various hearings might have been motivated by opposition to minority groups." Nevertheless, the Court also noted the lower court's conclusion that "evidence 'does not warrant the conclusion that this motivated the defendants.'" For its part, the lower court itself conceded that "the evidence shows that a multi-family development would seriously damage the value of the surrounding single-family homes and that its presence in the area is strongly opposed by large groups of citizens of the village. Their motive may well be opposition to minority or low-income groups, at least in part." But that court nevertheless concluded that "the evidence does not warrant the conclusion that this motivated the defendants."[15]

Let us consider these statements. In Chapter 6 I discussed the difficulties inherent in discerning an individual's—much less a multi-member body's—subjective intentions. In light of the evidence noted by the Supreme Court and the lower court in this case, we can now add to that difficulty the inherent ambiguity of a legislative record that may reflect bad motives—or may not. This ambiguity should not be surprising. Governmental decisions are messy. As we noted in Chapter 6, they are driven by a variety of motivations, often co-existing within the very same decision maker. The difficulty of reaching a conclusion we can confidently describe as the government's "intent" is made even more difficult when a court has to make judgments about that intent based on the inherently unruly record of a community hearing.

Consider, for example, courts' evaluation of the city's decision in the *Cleburne* case from Chapter 3. Recall the context of the zoning board's decision in *Cleburne*: Nearly one hundred residents crowded into a usually empty hearing room,[16] expressing both visceral fear and anger but also potentially more legitimate reasons for their opposition to the group home.[17] Indeed, the record of the city council's ultimate decision was so unclear that all the trial court could conclude was that neighbors' fears of the intellectually disabled was a factor that the town council "considered."

To be sure, the Court in *Arlington Heights* defined legislative history as the statements of the relevant decision makers, not as the statements of their constituents. Nevertheless, it is fair to impute to those decision makers at least some measure of the views of their constituents, especially in a context—such as those in *Arlington Heights* and *Cleburne*—where the decision was highly contested, where the constituents were vocal, and where the final decision was consistent with those constituent views. But this additional step—translating constituent statements into an intent we impute to those voters' representatives—just adds another layer of epistemic difficulty when courts attempt to determine the decision maker's intent from legislative history of this sort. It may be easier to infer intent when the statements in question come from the decision makers themselves, rather than those to whom they are beholden. In that case, we have "only" the difficulties discussed in Chapter 6. But when, as is often the case, local decisions are made in a context of constituent agitation and pressure, the intent inquiry becomes even more complex.

Summing Up and Moving Forward: The *Arlington Heights* Factors and Animus

The factors discussed above constitute a set of commonsense indicators to help courts discover when a facially neutral law in fact reflects potentially invidious discriminatory intent. They are not perfect; each has its limitations. But considered as a whole, they reflect a workable, straightforward methodology for reaching plausible conclusions about the intent of a government decision maker in taking a particular action. At the very least they reflect a reasonable and credible approach to that question. At least so thought seven of the eight justices who decided *Arlington Heights*—those seven justices expressed agreement with these factors, with the eighth justice declining to reach that question.[18]

At this point one might conclude that, if these factors are the appropriate ones for discerning the existence of discriminatory intent, then they should also be the factors used to identify animus. And that is correct—up to a point. As commonsense guideposts for determining when facially innocent government action raises discriminatory red flags, these factors indeed are very useful to the animus inquiry. But now we need to step back and examine the larger picture. In particular, we need to consider the relationship between discriminatory intent and animus. The *Arlington Heights* factors do in fact help us make credible determinations about discriminatory intent. But, as I cautioned earlier in this chapter, discriminatory intent itself is not the same as animus—not as a matter of logic and not as a matter of legal doctrine. What this means is that our use of those factors must be tweaked to account for the fact that, when we are searching for animus, we are searching for something different than discriminatory intent. The *Arlington Heights* discriminatory intent factors are the right tools. But when we examine a government action for animus, we are constructing a house with a slightly different floorplan. Thus those tools must be used in support of a different blueprint. The next chapter explains how the animus floorplan is different.

8

The Doctrinal Uniqueness of Animus

Absent searching judicial inquiry into the justification for . . . race-based measures, there is simply no way of determining what classifications are "benign" . . . and what classifications are in fact motivated by illegitimate notions of racial inferiority or simple racial politics. Indeed, the purpose of strict scrutiny is to "smoke out" illegitimate uses of race.
—*City of Richmond v. J. A. Croson Co.* (1989)

The short of it is that requiring the permit in this case appears to us to rest on an irrational prejudice against the mentally retarded.
—*City of Cleburne v. Cleburne Living Center* (1985)

So far, Part II of the book has focused on tools. Chapter 6 dispensed with the idea that our search for animus could start and end with an examination of the subjective mind-set of the lawmakers who enacted the challenged law. Chapter 7 supplemented that very limited tool with a set of commonsense factors that help us uncover discriminatory legislative action without having to play mind reader. Those factors serve as additional tools. With our hammers and saws laid out, it is time to unroll the doctrinal blueprint to see just what we are seeking to build.

The Consequences of Discriminatory Intent

Let's begin this process by considering the implications of an *Arlington Heights*–type inquiry. Recall that that inquiry ultimately seeks to determine whether a government action was motivated by a desire to discriminate on the ground claimed by the plaintiff. What would be the implication of a conclusion that the plaintiff had in fact made that showing—that he had proven, in other words, that the defendant's action was motivated by an intent to discriminate on the alleged ground—for example, on the basis of race? Intuitively, we would think that that would be the end of the case. After all, isn't "discrimination"—in particular, race "discrimination"—wrong? But as I noted in Chapter 7, the answer—at least as a constitutional matter—is "no." A conclusion that the state has "discriminated"—that is, that it has intentionally classified on the basis of race—simply triggers the relevant level of judicial scrutiny.

A moment's reflection should make clear the logic of this perhaps non-intuitive statement. Today, it is settled law that government may use race as a classification tool in at least some limited circumstances. In 2003 and 2016, for example, the Court held that, respectively, the University of Michigan Law School and the University of Texas undergraduate college could use race as a factor in deciding whether or not to admit an applicant.[1] Over a decade before the Michigan case, in a seminal case dealing with the allocation of city construction contracts, a majority of the Court also stated that under some limited circumstances government could use race in allocating such contracts. In that case the Court found that the City of Richmond, Virginia, had not justified its use of race and had not cabined its use of race carefully enough.[2] But the important point here—reinforced by the Michigan Law School case—is that sometimes government can constitutionally use race as a decisional criterion. Not often, and only with care. But theoretically, it can.

What this means is that "race discrimination" or, more precisely, a government intent to classify based on race, is not always unconstitutional.[3] The same applies to conclusions that government intended to classify on other grounds. For example, if a fire department insists that firefighters be of a certain height or weight, a woman might challenge such a facially sex-neutral policy as being motivated by a desire to exclude women. If the court agrees with the plaintiff, then, as with the race example, the next step is not simply to strike the law down. Instead, the next step is to apply to that law whatever scrutiny of sex classifications is appropriate. The law might fail that scrutiny, or it might survive it. (Today, in fact, it would likely fail it.) But the point is, that extra step—the application of that scrutiny—is a necessary part of the analysis.

Discriminatory Intent, Animus, and Class Legislation

That extra step might not be necessary or even justified when the plaintiff's claim is based on animus. The argument here is straightforward: Animus is itself a constitutional violation. Unlike race or sex or any other kind of classification, which triggers some level of judicial scrutiny—stringent, lenient, or something in between—a conclusion that a government action is based on animus should be fatal to a law or other government action. Recall the Court's conclusion from *Cleburne*, quoted (for a second time) at the start of this chapter: "The short of it is that requiring the permit in this case appears to us to rest on an irrational prejudice against the mentally retarded."[4] That statement was, by itself, enough to decide the case without any further judicial scrutiny. While this argument may be straightforwardly stated, proving it requires some work. The rest of this chapter will engage in that work.

This argument rests on an understanding of animus as the modern equivalent of factional, or class, legislation. As Chapter 1 explained, "class legislation" was the term nineteenth-century courts gave to legislation that, rather than pursuing legitimate governmental ends, instead aimed at benefiting or burdening such private groups. By the Civil War the class legislation concept was deeply entrenched in American legal thinking. Indeed, one of the most important congressional proponents of the Fourteenth Amendment described it as a bar on all such legislation.[5]

The class legislation concept rested on a foundation as old as the founding and as prominent as James Madison. Recall, again from Chapter 1, that that idea rested on Madison's fear of what he called "faction," which he defined in Federalist No. 10 as "a number of citizens, whether amounting to a majority or a minority of the whole, who are united and actuated by some common impulse of passion, or interest, adverse to the rights of other citizens, or the permanent and aggregate interests of the community."

In the remainder of Federalist No. 10 Madison offered his solution to the problem of faction. But for our purposes what is more important is his definition of the concept itself. That concept provides us with the key insight that unalloyed majoritarianism is not adequate to protect rights. After all, he says, "majorities" can possess "interests" that are adverse to those of "the community." And when majorities act on those interests, he implies, something has gone wrong with the lawmaking process.

As Chapter 1 explained, nineteenth-century courts built on this idea to create a constitutional law jurisprudence that insisted that government act only in pursuit of "the community's" interest. And, again, because such community interests did not necessarily equate with the interests of a majority, this jurisprudence posited that an act of the majority—that is, legislation—was at least potentially at risk of being the unconstitutional expression of factional interests. As we saw in Chapter 1, this approach to judicial review took the form of an insistence that government action be properly grounded in the so-called police power—that is, the power to regulate for the public good.

But Chapter 1 also noted that police power jurisprudence ultimately foundered. In particular, courts found it difficult, and ultimately impossible, to credibly second-guess when the effect of a law as imposing special burdens or bestowing particular benefits constituted the necessary, if unfortunate, by-product of government's pursuit of a public interest, or the law's ultimate aim. (Recall the railroad liability cases discussed in that chapter.) Instead, in the

Carolene Products case of 1938, the Court stated that in the future it would presume that most laws did in fact pursue a legitimate public interest, except, it tentatively suggested, in limited situations, which it identified in a footnote—the famous "Footnote 4" of that opinion.[6] Those exceptions included situations in which the Court had reason to think that the political process did not allow all sides to fairly present their points of view about what the public interest required. In turn, one of those situations occurs when there is "prejudice against discrete and insular minorities." But even the default "rational basis" test inquired into whether the challenged law promoted (or, in the test's words, "was rationally related to") a legitimate—that is, a public-regarding—interest.

What all this suggests is that non-public regarding legislation is unconstitutional. It might be difficult for courts to fully enforce this rule, as courts discovered during the class legislation era. That difficulty might then lead courts to adopt rules of thumb, or mediating principles such as suspect class/tiered scrutiny review, as a method of at least partially enforcing this rule.[7] But neither that underlying difficulty nor courts' attempt to mitigate it detracts from the force of the rule itself, which is a straightforward application of both Madison's theory and the practice of judicial review for conformance with government's proper police power. And even though the "police power" era of constitutional jurisprudence has passed into history, the ultimate question that jurisprudence sought to answer in a given case remains: Does the challenged government action reflect a constitutionally legitimate attempt to pursue the public interest? When a court can determine directly that a law fails that requirement, further scrutiny—heightened or otherwise—is unnecessary.

Tiered Scrutiny and the Public Purpose Requirement

In some situations, however, such further scrutiny—indeed, quite careful scrutiny—may be necessary. Such scrutiny is justified in situations where there's reason to think that the political process is unresponsive to the group the challenged law has burdened. In particular, Justice Harlan Fiske Stone, the author of Footnote 4, identified "prejudice against a discrete and insular minority" as "a special condition" that renders the political process unresponsive in this way. In turn, that unresponsiveness—the process's inability to account for the interests of the group that ends up bearing whatever burdens the statute imposes—raises the specter of legislation that simply seeks to burden that group for its own sake.

To be sure, there are other ways of thinking about the implications of such a political process breakdown. If one believes that legislation is simply a commodity bought and sold in an unprincipled political market where competing interests jostle and compromise simply to obtain their own preferred outcomes, then an exclusionary process is problematic for a different reason: because it disables one interest from participating in that marketplace rough-and-tumble. However, given American law's long and deep insistence that any government action at least seek to achieve a public-regarding goal,[8] it makes sense to understand the implications of a political process breakdown in terms of the resulting likelihood that the excluded group will find itself the victim of (unconstitutional) self-serving legislation at the hands of the legislative majority.

However one conceptualizes the harm of exclusion from the political process, Footnote 4 eventually had significant impact on the Court's equal protection jurisprudence—but not in the ways one might think. Writing in 1938, Justice Stone apparently had racial and ethnic discrimination on his mind when he wrote about "prejudice against discrete and insular minorities" generating such exclusion;[9] ironically, though, the Court has almost never analyzed race discrimination issues through the lens of Footnote 4. However, during the 1970s, when the Court began to consider *other* types of discrimination as candidates for more robust judicial scrutiny, it experimented with using Footnote 4's political process analysis as the foundation for that expansion. Most notably, in 1973 Justice Brennan provided a detailed process-based argument for according "strict scrutiny" to sex classifications. That argument attracted only four votes—and while a majority of the Court eventually adopted heightened scrutiny for sex classifications, it did not base that scrutiny explicitly on process-based grounds. However, during this same era the Court *did* use process-based language to consider according heightened judicial protection to classifications based on a variety of statuses, such as legitimacy and citizenship.[10]

As a practical matter, this period of experimentation ended in 1985 with the *Cleburne* case discussed in Chapter 3. Recall from that discussion that, even though the Court denied heightened scrutiny to the plaintiff group in that case (the intellectually disabled), it nevertheless ruled in its favor on the ground that the city's denial of the plaintiff's group home permit was grounded in animus. Now that we have a sense of the connection between tiered scrutiny/political process analysis, the underlying requirement that government action seek to promote a public interest, and, finally, the mirror image prohibition on government action based on purely private interests, we can understand the connection between *Cleburne*'s denial of suspect class status to the intellectually disabled and its animus conclusion. On this understanding, *Cleburne*'s conclusion about animus was an alternative way to answer the same question tiered scrutiny/political process analysis seeks to answer: Namely, is the government action in question grounded in a concern for the public good? In *Cleburne* the Court declined to answer that question through the path of holding the intellectually disabled to be a suspect class and thus according heightened scrutiny to the discrimination against it. Instead, it answered that question more directly—by holding, based on the evidence before it, that the city's decision was grounded in unconstitutional animus.[11]

Connecting Animus and Tiered Scrutiny

Let's pause and recap. I started this chapter by recalling what Chapter 7 established: The *Arlington Heights* factors constitute a commonsense set of factors to consider when deciding when a facially neutral government action reflects an intent to discriminate on a particular ground, for example, race or sex. I then suggested that, while these factors might also be useful to an investigation of animus, the two inquiries—into discriminatory intent and animus—are in fact quite different. They are different, I suggested, because while intent to discriminate on a particular ground may put the challenged law on precarious constitutional ground—if, for example, the intentional discrimination was based on sex—it does not necessarily doom the law. Instead, such discriminatory intent establishes that government has in fact discriminated (in the way the Constitution understands, that is, intentionally) against a given group (for example, against women). That conclusion in turn triggers the level of scrutiny that is ultimately based on *Carolene Products'* political-process-based analysis.

By contrast, our discussion of animus leads to a different result. That discussion—and in particular, its connection of animus to earlier notions of class legislation and even earlier notions of faction—revealed that, logically, a conclusion that a law was based on animus *does* doom a statute. No additional scrutiny required. Game over.

The Court has suggested precisely this analysis in some of its non-animus cases. For example, in *City of Richmond v. J.A. Croson Co.*,[12] the Court struck down Richmond, Virginia's race-based set-aside of a certain percentage of city contracts to minority-owned businesses. *Croson* is notable because it firmly established that even assertedly benign race classifications are subject to strict scrutiny, just like race classifications that were based in the bad old days of Jim Crow. One might well disagree with the Court's insistence on equating the level of scrutiny for these two types of laws; indeed, many persons have. But for now let us think about the logical implications of the Court's analysis.

In attempting to justify the Court's equivalent treatment of race-based affirmative action with Jim Crow laws, Justice O'Connor, *Croson*'s author, did not dispute that some government uses of race could in fact be benign and, thus, constitutional. But she argued that strict scrutiny was necessary to "smoke out" illegitimate uses of race—uses of race that were motivated either by what she called "illegitimate notions of racial inferiority or simple racial politics."[13] For our purposes, "simple racial politics" can be understood as equivalent to "factional politics"—that is, simple desires by one interest group (here, racial) to grab benefits for itself.[14] Such race-based factional politics, Justice O'Connor implied, was inherently unconstitutional. But race classifications themselves were not inherently unconstitutional—indeed, it was exactly to sift unconstitutional from constitutional uses of race that she insisted that *all* such classifications receive strict scrutiny.

But what if strict scrutiny—or heightened scrutiny more generally—is not workable? Recall *Cleburne*, from Chapter 3. In that case, the Court denied the intellectually disabled quasi-suspect status, in part because it did not think the group merited it. It also denied that status in part on concerns that courts could not competently apply it—that is, that courts could not easily distinguish between benign special treatment of the intellectually disabled and invidious discrimination. And finally, it denied that status in part because it thought that granting it would open the floodgates to other analogously situated groups seeking the same status. When political-process-based heightened scrutiny is not available, the Court implied, another approach would be to examine each particular instance of discrimination, to determine if it violated the core equal protection rule prohibiting animus-based action. And, of course, in *Cleburne*, it found that core rule to have been violated.

Animus analysis, therefore, can function as a substitute for the heightened scrutiny that is ultimately traceable to *Carolene Prod-*

ucts's Footnote 4. As in *Cleburne*, it might appropriately substitute for heightened scrutiny when a court feels incompetent to impose such heightened scrutiny to all classifications affecting that burdened group or when it feels that doing so would raise too many similar claims from analogously situated groups. Animus, in other words, is a way to short-circuit the heightened scrutiny that flows when government is held to have intentionally classified on the basis of some suspect or quasi-suspect classification. As Justice O'Connor explained in *Croson*, such heightened scrutiny is a way of "smoking out" unconstitutional motivations. Those unconstitutional motivations are exactly what are encapsulated in the concept of "animus." To use a simplistic analogy, a conclusion about animus is the equivalent of a go-to-jail card in the game Monopoly. The card does not say you stop somewhere else (that is, apply a level of scrutiny) on the way to jail. Instead, it says, "Go Directly to Jail." So, too, with animus. A court's conclusion that a given law reflects animus should mean "Do Not Stop to Apply a Particular Level of Scrutiny." Instead, the statute should go directly to jail.

Troubling Precedent

If you agree with the analysis up to now, you may be expecting the triumphant conclusion that, in fact, the Court's animus doctrine understands a finding of animus in exactly this way—as a "Go Directly to Jail" card that does not involve stopping along the way to apply a particular level of scrutiny. Unfortunately, candor compels the conclusion that the Court does not appear to do this. And so we need to think about whether this analysis—even if it is attractive—contains within it a fatal flaw, or at least a bug, or whether, instead, the Court just doesn't get it.

The first case we need to think about is the foundational case for modern animus jurisprudence—*Department of Agriculture v. Moreno*, the 1973 case discussed in Chapter 2 that coined the "bare desire to harm" language. In that case the Court, after quoting legislative history indicating Congress's motive in defining "household" as it did for purposes of food stamp eligibility, and after criticizing that motive as "a bare desire to harm" a politically unpopular group, nevertheless went on to consider other, more legitimate, justifications for the statutory definition. Thus *Moreno* suggested that a constitutionally illegitimate purpose—the "bare desire to harm" "hippies and hippie communes"—was not necessarily fatal to the statute. That suggestion, of course, raises serious questions about our earlier, tentative, conclusion that a finding of animus is necessarily fatal to a government action.

A good place to start our thinking about this is with the language of *Moreno* itself. Up to now I have elided a potentially important qualifier to the Court's "bare desire to harm" language. The key paragraph is set forth here in its entirety, except for citations to court cases and the legislative record:

> Thus, if it is to be sustained, the challenged classification must rationally further some legitimate governmental interest other than those specifically stated in the congressional "declaration of policy" [about the overall goals of the food stamp program, which the Court had concluded did not support the "household" definition law]. Regrettably, there is little legislative history to illuminate the purposes of the 1971 amendment of § 3(e). The legislative history that does exist, however, indicates that that amendment was intended to prevent so-called "hippies" and "hippie communes" from participating in the food stamp program. The challenged classification clearly cannot be sustained by reference to this congressional purpose. For if the constitutional conception of "equal protection of the laws" means anything, it must at the very least mean that a bare congressional desire to harm a politically unpopular group cannot constitute a *legitimate* governmental interest. As a result, *"(a) purpose to discriminate against hippies cannot, in and of itself and without reference to (some independent) considerations in the public interest,* justify the 1971 amendment."[15]

The key language here is the italicized phrase at the end, which is part of the Court's quotation from the lower court's opinion. Coming immediately after the sentence containing the famous "bare . . . desire to harm" language, that quotation referred to additional considerations—considerations "in the public interest"—as a necessary component of the statute, at least if the statute was going to be considered constitutional.

So far, this material supports the argument that, indeed, a statute may reflect animus but nevertheless may still be constitutional, as long as other "considerations in the public interest" exist. And indeed, the Court in *Moreno* then proceeded to consider the government's more legitimate-sounding arguments for the statutory definition—arguments about fraud detection and prevention. The Court found those arguments wanting, but for our purposes that is not the key fact here. Instead, the important point is that the Court suspected animus, concluded that such animus would be insufficient to support the constitutionality of the law, but then proceeded to consider more legitimate government justifications. This hardly seems like an argument that animus is a silver bullet that kills a statute immediately.

Other foundational animus cases reveal similar ambiguities about the status of animus as a necessarily fatal flaw in any statute or government action. In *Cleburne*, the Court's identification of the city council's responsiveness to constituents' dislike of the intellectually disabled did not stop the Court's analysis in its tracks. Instead, it continued on, considering more legitimate-sounding justifications for the council's permit denial (albeit with more skepticism than one would expect in ostensibly rational basis review). Thus, just like in *Moreno*, the Court's seeming identification of animus did not stop it from further examining the law.

Justice O'Connor's concurrence in *Lawrence* made explicit what seems to have been implied in both *Moreno* and *Cleburne*. Recall from Chapter 4 that in *Lawrence* she voted to strike down Texas's same-sex sodomy prohibition on equal protection grounds. Justice

O'Connor wrote the following in her separate concurrence: "When a law exhibits . . . a desire to harm a politically unpopular group, we have applied a more searching form of rational basis review to strike down such laws under the Equal Protection Clause." This statement seems to decide the question pretty conclusively: When a court finds animus ("a desire to harm a politically unpopular group") it does not just strike the law down. Instead, O'Connor described the Court's equal protection jurisprudence as having "applied a more searching form of rational basis review to strike down such laws." So much for the idea of animus as a doctrinal silver bullet.

Thus, contrary to our theory, the case law seems to support the proposition that a finding of animus is *not* sufficient to strike down a law. To be sure, the cases suggest that animus *is* enough to trigger heightened scrutiny, even if that scrutiny is ostensibly portrayed as simple application of the traditional, deferential, rational basis standard. But the scrutiny continues, even after the animus finding. That suggests, at least at first glance, that animus is not necessarily fatal to a statute.

To be sure, some scholars resist this conclusion. For example, Susannah Pollvogt, a prominent scholar of animus doctrine, argues that animus is in fact what she calls a doctrinal "silver bullet." At other times she argues that the presence of animus "poisons the well"[16] in the sense that it discredits other, more legitimate, justifications for a law. There is much to be said for the idea that animus is in fact fatal to a law's constitutionality. Indeed, this book promotes exactly that proposition. But, as attractive as that proposition is, it is incomplete. In particular, it elides the question of how one determines whether animus in fact exists. Indeed, in her most detailed treatment of the question, Pollvogt writes,

> In reality, when the Court identifies *evidence* of animus, it discredits the other purported state interests [justifying the challenged discrimination]. Thus, animus acts as a doctrinal silver bullet. This

is appropriate, because if animus is, indeed, constitutionally impermissible, no law found to be *based in animus* should be permitted
to stand.[17]

Consider the italicized words in that quote. There is a big difference between "evidence of animus" and a conclusion that a law
is "based in animus." That gap may in fact mirror the analogous
gap between the Court's seeming willingness to continue scrutinizing a law even after it uncovers evidence of animus and Pollvogt's
(normatively attractive) argument that animus is a "silver bullet." If
we are going to bridge this gap, we need to think more about how
we discover animus and how much evidence is sufficient for us to
conclude that it does in fact exist in a given case.

Other scholars have reached variants of this same tentative conclusion. For example, Dale Carpenter has argued that a law should
not be struck down as based in animus unless animus "materially influenced" the government decision in question.[18] Carpenter
makes the clearly correct observation that government decisions
are motivated by many considerations, especially when the decision is made by a multi-person institution such as a legislature. He
thus suggests that unconstitutional animus must strongly (in his
words, "materially") influence the decision before that decision is
fatally infected.

We can embrace a conclusion similar to Carpenter's, but
through a different route—one that has the potential of preserv-
ing the concept of animus as necessarily fatal—as Pollvogt's "silver
bullet." To repeat, there is good reason to find a path that harmonizes Pollvogt's conclusion that animus (however defined) should
be fatal to a statute with Carpenter's realization that the mixed motivations of government actors requires that we be careful in how
we identify animus. Constructing a doctrine in which animus is
necessarily fatal to a statute (or other government action) returns
some coherence to the Court's constitutional law jurisprudence. It
makes the animus doctrine more closely parallel to the nineteenth-

century Court's concern with class legislation. Closer to the present day, it also places animus on the same level as the *invidious* uses of race and other classification tools that the Court in cases like *Croson* identified as necessarily unconstitutional.

The challenge is to determine whether we can explain the animus cases as cases in which the Court was seeking to determine if animus really was motivating the law. On this theory, the Court's consideration of the government's alternative justifications for the challenged laws could be understood as reflecting the Court's search for the government's ultimate motivation in enacting the law. If so, then these cases exhibit yet another parallel with the Court's discriminatory intent doctrine—just like the intent cases, the animus cases are fundamentally about a search for the government's intent.

Thus, before we concede that these cases reject our nascent idea that animus is in fact a per se constitutional wrong, we should think about whether the Court in these cases really was *searching* for animus and was indeed ready and willing to strike a law down once it found it—whether it was ready to fire the silver bullet, but only after it knew that it had the right target in its sights. Perhaps the Court, either without knowing it or just without saying it, was doing what it normally does when it seeks to uncover the intent lurking behind a facially innocuous government action.

9

The Elusive Search for Animus

Proof that the decision by the Village was motivated
in part by a racially discriminatory purpose would
not necessarily have required invalidation of the
challenged decision. Such proof would, however, have
shifted to the Village the burden of establishing that
the same decision would have resulted even had the
impermissible purpose not been considered.
—*Village of Arlington Heights v. Metropolitan Housing
Development Corp.* (1977)

Chapter 6 explained why our most intuitive understanding of
animus—as subjective ill will—does not provide a fully workable
methodology for courts to uncover it. Chapter 7 introduced a set
of commonsense factors, borrowed from a related constitutional
law doctrine—the doctrine of discriminatory intent—and suggested that those factors could help courts in the search for the
analogous phenomenon of animus.

Chapter 8 noted a limitation to that analogy: Unlike a finding
of discriminatory intent, a finding of animus should conclusively
decide the case against the constitutionality of the challenged government action. It made this argument as a matter of logic and
conformance with the class legislation heritage of animus doctrine.
But Chapter 8 also added a troubling note. It identified several of
the foundational animus opinions the Court or individual justices
have written as having suggested that judicial review should con-
tinue even after the court identified animus. Those calls for further scrutiny even after the Court identified animus suggest that

animus is not a doctrinal "silver bullet." In turn, that conclusion poses serious problems for our attempt to connect animus to older notions of class legislation.

Chapter 8 concluded by offering a solution to this conundrum. It may be that a court's continued search for a legitimate foundation for an action found to have been motivated in part by animus actually reflects a search for the ultimate intention behind that action. In other words, it may be that animus really is a doctrinal silver bullet. But conclusively identifying animus may require searching for other possible explanations for the challenged law. This chapter examines how that search should be undertaken.

Burden Shifting in the Intent Inquiry

This argument requires us to return to our discussion of the intent inquiry in equal protection law. After all, what we are talking about in this chapter is how best to identify animus. Given that we are using the same tools as the intent inquiry (that is, the *Arlington Heights* factors we introduced in Chapter 7), it makes sense to consider how discriminatory intent jurisprudence actually uses those tools. Once we understand how the intent inquiry uses them, we can consider whether such uses can be directly transferred into the animus inquiry or whether we need to tweak that doctrine to account for our different context.

The intent inquiry involves two stages of argumentation and proof. First, the plaintiff is required to show, using the *Arlington Heights* factors, that an intent to discriminate on the alleged ground was *a* motivating factor. Note the italicized word in that last sentence. The plaintiff is not required to show that the alleged intent was the sole, or even the predominant, motivator of the challenged government action. Instead, the plaintiff need only show that that intent was one motivation.

But if the plaintiff makes that showing, that is not the end of the case. Instead, the burden then shifts to the government defendant to show that it would have made that same decision, even in the absence of the discriminatory intent that the plaintiff has just proven constituted part of the government's motivation. (This part of the *Arlington Heights* opinion is quoted at the start of this chapter.) If the government can show that, indeed, it would have made that same decision even had its motivations been completely pure, then the court will hold that there was no intent to discriminate on the alleged ground. But if it cannot make that showing, then what we have is a case of intentional discrimination on the basis alleged by the plaintiff.

A simple example will both illustrate this idea and reveal its foundation in common sense. Recall our firefighter hypothetical from Chapter 8, in which a fire department has a rule requiring that firefighters be of a certain height. One might expect that this rule would disqualify more women than men, given the statistical reality that, on average, men are taller than women. Suppose that a woman sues the fire department, alleging that the rule "discriminates" on the basis of sex. "Discriminates" is in quotation marks because I am using that term in its legal sense. In a very basic way, the rule clearly "discriminates" against women, in that it has the effect of disqualifying more women than men. But since the Equal Protection Clause prohibits only intentional discrimination, such disparate effects are usually not enough by themselves to establish "discrimination" in the constitutional sense.[1]

Under standard equal protection doctrine, the female plaintiff in our hypothetical would shoulder the burden in the first phase of the intent inquiry. As explained above, her burden would consist of showing that the fire department's height rule was motivated, *in part*, by an intent to classify based on sex. She would not have to show that it was the only factor motivating the rule, or even the main factor motivating it—she would just have to show that it was one of the motivations. If she succeeded, then the burden would shift to the fire department. At that point it would have been held that the department had sex at least partly in mind when it promulgated the height rule. When confronted with such a finding, the department would face a new hurdle: It would have to show that it would still have promulgated that rule even if—now, contrary to the court's finding—it never had a sexist bone in its institutional body. In essence, the department would have to prove that height was a consideration that, independent of its correlation with sex, prompted the department to promulgate the regulation.

Consider the common sense of this burden-shifting framework.[2] It would be unfairly burdensome on a plaintiff, such as the woman in this case, to prove that sex was the complete or even just the primary motivating factor in a case such as this. Even with the ability to review the department's records, proving that sex was the only or the primary motivating factor would be difficult. More conceptually, the reality that institutions usually act based on a variety of motives makes it unfair to insist that she prove that the department acted *only* out of a sex discriminatory motivation. Still, because she is the plaintiff, it is fair to require that she offer at least some proof of the fire department's intent—at least if we assume, as we are here, that intent is a constitutional requirement.[3] But it is also fair to shift the burden to the fire department if the plaintiff shows that sex was at least one of the things the department was thinking about when it promulgated the rule. After all, the department is best situated to prove its own motivations.

Finally, consider the reasonableness of the ultimate conclusions this framework yields. If the fire department cannot prove that it would have made the same decision even absent the sex discrimination intent, then it is fair to say that the woman has in fact been the victim of sex discrimination.[4] In that case, she has suffered a burden "because of" the department's intent to classify on that ground. Conversely, if the department does manage to carry its burden, then the woman cannot in fairness be said to have been the victim of sex discrimination. In that latter case, the woman is simply the victim of a decision motivated by a conclusion that, in fact, fire fighters really do need to be of a certain height. In that case, she would still be the victim of height discrimination (although that would likely not help her much in court, given the constitutionally non-suspect status of height). But not sex discrimination.

Mapping Burden-Shifting onto the Animus Inquiry

Let's now map this structure onto the animus inquiry. As applied to that inquiry, the discriminatory intent burden-shifting framework would require some explanation from the government if the plaintiff can demonstrate that animus was a factor in the challenged government action. Thus, for example, if the plaintiff can convince a court that a law's severe disparate impact implies simple dislike or disapproval of the burdened group, or if the plaintiff can show that the government's decisional process leading to enactment of the challenged law was explicitly infected with animus, then it might be appropriate for a court to seek an explanation from the government. In the intent context, that explanation would take the form of a government showing that, as with the fire department's height rule, the government would have made the same decision even had it lacked the alleged discriminatory intent the plaintiff succeeded in suggesting. In the context of the animus inquiry, that explanation would take an analogous form. It would require that government demonstrate that legitimate needs motivated the government's action.

But note something interesting about this parallel. In both situations, the burden rests with the government. In the intent context the government must *demonstrate* that it would have made the same decision even absent the discriminatory intent. Similarly, in the animus context the government would have to *demonstrate* that legitimate needs motivated the challenged action. Of course, in the intent context this placement of the burden on the government occurs before any particular level of equal protection scrutiny is performed—indeed, the entire question at this stage is whether the court actually has before it a case of, say, sex discrimination. Only after it decides that it does would the court apply the appropriate level of heightened scrutiny.

The situation is slightly different in the animus context. In the animus context, this burden shifting occurs *as part of* the application of the relevant scrutiny level. Do not forget that in these cases we are dealing with explicit classifications on the challenged ground—disability, sexual orientation, and so forth. Thus, a court would immediately turn to application of the relevant scrutiny level—usually rational basis, since the very reason courts need to worry about animus is that heightened scrutiny is, for whatever reason, deemed inappropriate. Once we realize this, then we realize that the burden shifting we have been talking about has to occur as part of the rational basis scrutiny itself. And when we realize, as we did a few paragraphs above, that part of that burden shifting involves placing proof burdens on the government, we can start to understand why, even under rational basis review, the Court has sometimes placed the burden of explanation on the government. For example, the *Cleburne* Court explicitly placed that burden on the government when it noted the lack of evidence in the record justifying the government's argument that the group home's population density was inappropriate for the neighborhood. Such a placement of the burden may sound inconsistent with rational basis review—indeed, Justice Marshall lodged exactly this objection in his partial dissent in *Cleburne*. But it makes sense, once we realize both the parallel between the animus inquiry and the intent inquiry and the lack of complete equivalence between the two.

Reconciling the Cases

This understanding of animus reconciles the troubling precedent we identified in Chapter 8. Recall that in a number of animus cases we have studied the Court did not stop when it encountered evidence of animus. In *Moreno* the Court fretted over the troubling legislative history behind the food stamp law's definition of households (the statements about "hippies" and "hippie communes") but nevertheless went on to consider other, more legitimate justifications for the law. In *Cleburne* the Court noted the city's argument that it denied the intellectually disabled group a zoning permit because of constituents' dislike and fear of that group, but, like *Moreno*, it nevertheless continued on to consider other more constitutionally palatable justifications for that denial. Finally, in *Lawrence*, Justice O'Connor explicitly stated that "a bare . . . desire to harm a politically unpopular group" triggered, not an immediate strike-down, but instead closer judicial review. When I summarized these facets of those cases in the last chapter, I noted the problem they posed for any theory that considered animus a per se constitutional violation.

But now that we understand how animus is found, those cases fit neatly into our theory. If those cases' more careful scrutiny and consideration of alternative, more legitimate, justifications for laws constitute part of the search for animus itself, then we can still say that animus does indeed constitute a doctrinal "silver bullet." But *the process of finding* animus requires that we give the government a chance to prove that something else was really motivating the government. Just as the intent inquiry gives the government (for example, the fire department in our hypothetical) the chance to prove that it would have taken the challenged action (that is, the height rule) even absent the alleged intent (that is, to discriminate on the basis of sex), so, too, the search for animus gives the government a chance to prove that it really was not motivated by animus. But again, that latter inquiry is part of rational basis review itself, as illustrated by rational basis cases such as *Cleburne*, rather than an inquiry into "discriminatory intent" per se.

Other scholars have reached similar, but not identical, conclusions. For example, Dale Carpenter has argued that a law should be struck down if animus is found to have "materially influenced" the government's decision to enact it. As noted in my earlier reference to his argument, there is good wisdom in acknowledging that government bodies, especially multi-member bodies such as legislatures, usually have multiple motivations for their actions. Thus there is likewise good wisdom in recognizing that a smidgen of animus should probably not suffice to fatally infect a statute. The only questions then become, (1) How much animus is enough to cause that fatal infection? and (2) How do we structure the evidentiary inquiry? The "how much" question is addressed in the next chapter. Our discussion up to now concerns the structuring of that inquiry. That discussion suggests that the burden-shifting structure borrowed from other equal protection doctrines provides an approach that is both logical (because it asks the right question: whether the law was enacted "because of"[5] animus) and normatively attractive (because it harmonizes the animus line of equal protection doctrine with its more completely worked-out discriminatory intent cousin).

Where the Parallel Stops

Still, this harmonization is incomplete: As I have noted, in the animus context the burden-shifting structure I have been describing occurs within the framework of rational basis review, rather than as part of a preliminary inquiry into discriminatory intent. This difference may well strike readers as a trivial detail. One might object that, as a practical matter, the animus inquiry I have been sketching out is the exact same as the intent inquiry. Both require the plaintiff to make an initial showing that something troubling is lurking in the challenged law. Neither requires the plaintiff to show that that something is the efficient, or but-for, cause of the challenged law. And finally, if the plaintiff does make that initial showing, both inquiries require the government to prove that it was really motivated by benign purposes.

But there is a difference, and it matters. As Chapter 8 explained, a finding of discriminatory intent is different from a finding of animus. A finding of such intent—even an intent to discriminate on a presumptively unconstitutional ground such as race—simply triggers the relevant standard of review. To be sure, that review may well be quite stringent—as it is, for example, in the case of race itself. But, at least ostensibly and, indeed, even in practice, that review may not lead to the (intentional) race classification being struck down.[6] By contrast, the animus conclusion—once the Court reaches it—does in fact lead to the law's demise.

This distinction reflects the fact that animus is, on its own, a constitutional wrong. Not a presumptive wrong, subject to possible validation if the Court finds a compelling reason for the animus. Instead, as a per se matter, there can be no legitimate reason for an action taken out of animus. By insisting on this rule, we can clarify constitutional law jurisprudence by tying the modern Court's animus doctrine to prior generations' focus on class legislation and the framing generation's focus on "faction" as the primary risk posed by majoritarian legislation. Indeed, it bears noting that the foundation for modern animus doctrine—*Moreno*—spoke of "a bare . . . desire to harm *a politically powerless minority.*" When we remember that James Madison expressed concern that democratic governance raised the risk of *majoritarian* oppression, we can draw a further connection between animus and the idea of faction.

The Value of Animus Doctrine

It is worth the effort to draw this connection. Animus doctrine requires a strong, coherent doctrinal foundation in order to avoid serious conceptual and practical problems. First, its seeming imputation of bad subjective motivation raises difficult practical problems about proof—the problems we identified in Chapter 6. In turn, those problems exposed an even deeper practical, or perhaps political, problem that flows from defining animus subjectively: the problem of accusing a legislature, and even voters directly, of harboring and acting out of a subjective dislike of a particular group of their fellow citizens.

To be sure, the "animus" label, whatever the process by which it is affixed, carries with it some stigma of impropriety: however one slices it, labeling an action as motivated by animus necessarily suggests some type of improper motivation. Some scholars have cited that fact to criticize the entire concept of animus, even while favoring the results that doctrine reaches. One has described judicial conclusions of animus as "insulting and disrespectful," while another scholar places the entire concept of animus in a category of judicial name calling he labels a "jurisprudence of denigration."[7] Some justices have leveled similar criticisms. In particular, recall that Justice Scalia began his dissent in *Romer v. Evans* (the Colorado Amendment 2 case) by accusing the Court of mistaking a (constitutionally valid) "cultural struggle" with a (constitutionally invalid) "fit of spite."[8] More colorfully, in *Windsor* (the Defense of Marriage Act case) he accused the majority of viewing members of Congress as "unhinged members of a wild-eyed lynch mob."[9]

This objection can be overstated—at any rate, it is not unique to animus. For example, the concern about stigmatizing legislatures and voters has not stopped the Court from insisting that equal protection plaintiffs prove "discriminatory intent." While this latter concept may not carry the full moral implications of a finding of "animus," it nevertheless surely tars the challenged government action with some taint of moral impropriety.

Still, we can concede that a finding of "animus" stings—perhaps even more than a finding of "discriminatory intent." But heeding these calls to abandon reliance on an animus theory threatens to discard a concept that can play a useful role in constitutional law. Despite any reasonable concerns about inflaming the culture wars by accusing one side of acting in ways that suggest a "lynch mob," the fact of the matter is that animus plays a necessary and historically supported role in American constitutional law.

It is necessary because the enormous diversity of American society and complexity of American government make it more difficult than perhaps it used to be to conclude that any use of a particular classification trait is always necessarily suspect. Today, government makes a vast variety of decisions, at levels ranging from neighborhood councils and local agencies and boards to the Congress of the United States, on issues affecting nearly every type of human activity in which Americans engage. Such decisions necessarily involve classifying persons. The ubiquity of government classification matters because today, across any relevant axis—religion, ethnicity, lifestyle, socioeconomic class—American society is probably more diverse today than it has ever been. That diversity makes it more difficult than ever to judge all governmental classifications according to a rigid, three-tiered structure.

But an even deeper problem lurks. The crumbling of older binaries—black/white, Catholic/Protestant, and today, even male/female—makes it even more difficult for courts to engage in the categorization that serves as the first step in tiered scrutiny analysis. To be sure, classification tools—for example, race, sex, or sexual orientation—may ostensibly remain manageable. But to the extent such tools have historically been wielded with a solid understanding of what they mean and who is affected, such confidence may be eroding. For example, until recent decades it was relatively clear that "sex discrimination" meant discrimination against either women or men. Today, however, the term "sex" is far more shaded, involving, at least potentially, transgender persons (of various transition stages), intersexed persons, and, depending on one's understanding of "sex discrimination," even gays and lesbians.[10] This is not to say that such developments make government action more likely to be constitutional. But it *is* to say that decisions about the constitutionality of a particular government action may have to be made at more granular, particularistic levels. The concept of animus can play an important role in making such granular decisions.

Indeed, we know that animus plays such a role because we have always known it. This raises the second point made above, about the historical groundedness of the idea of animus. At least since James Madison's time, American political thinkers have recognized that democratic self-governance inevitably raises the danger of majoritarian self-dealing. Groups—"factions" in Madison's terminology—may seek political power, not to promote their conception of the public good, but simply to further their own parochial interests. Of course, as I have noted several times already, the Court eventually realized that it could not easily distinguish such parochial concerns from conceptions of the public good that simply happened to benefit a certain group. A lower tax rate for capital gains income might well promote the interests of a particular class, but such a tax policy might also promote the public good. At the very least, courts have no special competence to decide such questions.

But what courts *can* do is investigate motivations. Again, discerning subjective motivations sometimes remains beyond a court's competence. However, sometimes, as in *Moreno* and *Cleburne*, such intent might be relatively plainly visible. If not, as in *Romer*, it might be inferable from the larger context of the challenged law. In cases such as these, it is not only appropriate for courts to strike down the government action, but it is also consistent with Madison's concern with faction and with nineteenth-century courts' concern with class legislation. In other words, when courts embrace animus, even in its indirectly proven form, they embrace a principle that has animated American constitutional jurisprudence since the founding.

The Next Steps

Let's take stock. I have now suggested an approach to animus that recognizes both its logical connection to the intent inquiry but also its lack of complete equivalency. The complex relationship between animus doctrine and the intent inquiry—related, but not identical—rests in part on logic: the conceptual incorrectness of concluding that an animus finding, just like a finding of intent to discriminate on a suspect ground, simply triggers heightened judicial scrutiny. But it also rests on history: in particular, the opportunity to connect animus doctrine to firmly grounded constitutional concerns about class legislation and, even earlier in our history, about "factions" in a democracy.

We have now gone even farther. We have recognized that often the Court's animus cases do in fact treat concerns about animus as simply a trigger for heightened scrutiny, rather than as a reason to stop the analysis immediately and rule for the plaintiffs. We were able to explain that seeming anomaly by noting that those cases' heightened scrutiny can again be helpfully analogized to standard equal protection intent analysis—in particular, the component of the intent inquiry in which, after the plaintiff shows that the alleged intent played at least some role in the challenged decision, the burden shifts to the government to demonstrate that it would have made the same decision even absent that allegedly invidious intent.

I argued that such burden shifting is analogous to the heightened scrutiny courts apply in animus cases. In both cases, the goal is to figure out what is really motivating the government. But the searches proceed differently. In the intent context, that search is conducted by forcing the government to explain itself when the plaintiff proves that the alleged intent was a motivating factor in the government's decision. In particular, when the plaintiff makes such a showing the burden shifts to the government to explain that other, non-discriminatory, purposes motivated the action the plaintiff claims is motivated by an intent to classify on the alleged ground (for example, race). Only *after* intent is established is the proper (heightened) level of scrutiny applied. By contrast, in the animus context, discovery of the government's real motivation is accomplished *through the means of* heightened rational basis scrutiny that features a requirement that government affirmatively justify its action. In a very real sense, then, the animus inquiry folds the burden-shifting step into the heightened scrutiny step. If the government fails that combined step, then it loses—just as it loses if, in the standard intent inquiry, at step 1 it fails to convince the court that it would have made the same decision absent the alleged intent and then, at step 2, it also fails the resultant heightened scrutiny. Thus, the inquiries are very similar, but in standard equal protection analysis the inquiry proceeds in two steps, rather than in one as in animus cases.

All good work—at least, I hope that the reader thinks so. But we are left with two immensely practical, and immensely difficult, questions. First, in an animus case, how should courts go about determining when to use more careful scrutiny? In other words, when should courts suspect animus, with the result that they subject challenged laws to more careful scrutiny to confirm its presence? Second, what should that heightened scrutiny look like? Again, these are practical questions. The first one essentially addresses the question of how convincing the plaintiff has to be that animus may lurk behind the challenged law. The second one asks what a court is supposed to do when the plaintiff succeeds in raising that suspicion. Chapter 10 takes up both of these issues, before Chapter 11 applies what we have learned to concrete examples.

How Much Animus Is Enough? And What Should We Do about It?

Because in our view the record does not reveal any
rational basis for believing that the Featherston home
would pose any special threat to the city's legitimate
interests, we affirm the judgment below insofar as it
holds the ordinance invalid as applied in this case.
—*City of Cleburne v. Cleburne Living Center* (1985)

In this chapter we come to practicalities. How much proof, and of what sort, should a court require when deciding whether a particular government action is deemed to carry with it the taint of animus? And how should courts respond to that taint? In answering these questions we cannot be satisfied with generalities and concepts, as, frankly, we have been up to this point. Such generalities have their place—indeed, they are necessary when sketching the outlines of the argument. But now we have the theoretical blueprint. It's time to build the structure.

How Much Evidence Is Enough?

Let us begin by considering the first question. As we have before, we can find some helpful hints in the factors the *Arlington Heights* Court identified as relevant to a court's inquiry into whether a plaintiff has established that alleged discriminatory intent played at least some role in the challenged decision. Recall those factors: the extent and foreseeability of the disparate impact the decision created, the historical background of the decision, the more recent and specific sequence of events leading up to the decision, officials' statements and other legislative history, and the extent to which the challenged decision was marked by procedural or substantive deviations from normal practice.

In applying those factors, the Court has often, if not always, been flexible, refusing to insist on the presence of some particular number of these factors or some particular weight to be assigned any one of them. Indeed, in 1982 the Court concluded, quite logically, that a finding of discriminatory intent was a factual one, rather than a legal one.[1] That conclusion has the effect of rendering the intent determination one primarily made by the federal trial court, the court that actually heard the testimony and whose judge actually lives in the community where the alleged discrimination occurred. In turn, that understanding suggests that intent is not uncovered through a mechanical process that can predictably replicate similar results when faced with ostensibly similar inputs. Rather, as a fact issue, intent requires a sensitivity to context, in particular, how those facts interrelate to create a result that we call "discriminatory intent" or the lack thereof.

This may sound vague. And indeed, intent inquiries *are* vague, to the extent they cannot be mechanically analyzed or applied with consistent results, as can, for example, a chemical formula. To reinforce this point, let us recall two examples we considered earlier, in Chapter 7. First, in *Reitman v. Mulkey*,[2] the Court held that California violated the Equal Protection Clause when its voters amended the state constitution to bestow upon property owners the right to sell their property to whomever they wished and for whatever reason and thus repealed fair housing laws the state legislature had previously enacted.

As Chapter 7 explained, *Reitman* was not a case about the intent requirement per se, and much less about animus doctrine, both of which were formally introduced into constitutional doctrine only years later. But it raises an analogous issue, given the ambiguous nature of the California voters' decision. On the one hand, the effect of Proposition 14 was simply to repeal those earlier fair housing laws—laws that no state was under an obligation to enact in the first place and, thus, laws that a state was free to enact and then repeal if it so chose. But the California supreme court saw it another way, as (unconstitutionally) involving the state with private discrimination. In affirming the California court's conclusion, the Supreme Court noted approvingly that the state court had "assessed the ultimate impact of [Proposition 14] in the California environment" and concluded that the amendment in fact did unconstitutionally implicate the state in that private discrimination.

Reitman is relevant for our current purposes because it illustrates the necessarily non-formulaic nature of any inquiry into intent. To repeat, *Reitman* was not explicitly a case about discriminatory intent. But in asking whether Proposition 14 "encourage[d] and significantly involve[d]" the state in private discrimination, the *Reitman* Court was asking an analogous question: How should we understand that law—not just its effects, but its deeper meaning? The Court's recognition that answering that question requires understanding "the California environment"—that is, the factual and political context surrounding the law's enactment—reflects the necessarily impressionistic, holistic approach that would later mark cases that addressed the intent issue more explicitly.

To see this dynamic in the intent context, let's consider our second example—*Arlington Heights* itself. Recall that that case, after setting forth the factors relevant to the intent inquiry, then proceeded to apply those factors to the facts before it. The facts concerned a not-for-profit housing corporation's desire to erect on a particular plot of land multi-family, low-income housing that would likely be racially integrated and the city's denial of a zoning variance that would allow the project to be built. Applying the factors it had just set forth, the *Arlington Heights* Court found no discriminatory intent.

The Court began by acknowledging the racially disparate impact of the decision. But it noted that the city had historically been "undeniably committed" to single-family housing as its dominant residential land use and that the decision was procedurally regular—indeed, if anything, the city gave the zoning request unusually careful consideration. Finally, it concluded that the statements made by the relevant government decision makers focused "almost exclusively on the zoning aspects" of the variance request.[3]

The sense one gets from the Court's analysis is that the zoning decision appeared to the Court to be fundamentally non-race based. To be sure, the Court acknowledged the racially disparate impact of the decision. It also took note of the trial court's conclusion that, in the (Supreme) Court's words, "some of the opponents of Lincoln Green who spoke at the various hearings might have been motivated by opposition to minority groups." Nevertheless, the Court did not think that the evidence warranted overturning both lower courts' conclusions that the challenged decision lacked discriminatory intent. It did not reach that conclusion because it consciously weighed the disparate impact against the other factors or because it used some explicit balancing formula. Rather, the sense one gets from the Court—a sense borne out by its later description of the intent inquiry as a factual one—is that the Court envisioned the factors it identified as guideposts in a holistic, contextualized evaluative process.[4] It is exactly such a contextualized process that also applies when a court determines "how much" animus is necessary before a court applies heightened rational basis review.

Nevertheless, as we have discussed earlier, factors either identical or analogous to the intent factors identified in *Arlington Heights* clarify the task, at least somewhat. As we saw in Part I when we examined the Court's animus cases, the Court has found an animus-based trigger for more careful rational basis review based on legislative history (*Moreno*), evidence about the specific sequence of events leading up to the challenged decision (*Cleburne*), the extent of the impact on the burdened group (*Romer* and *Windsor*), and deviations from the normal substance of government decision making in that area (*Romer* and *Windsor*). Just as with the intent inquiry from which these factors are drawn, the Court's use of these factors in the animus inquiry does not reflect a mechanical jurisprudence that purports to weigh these factors or even to count up the number of them that appear in any given case. Still, the identification of such factors helps sharpen what would otherwise be a wholly impressionistic inquiry.

Furthermore, animus is—or should be seen as—such an unusual occurrence that cases alleging it should feature relatively extreme instances of these factors. Surely, the cases decided by the Supreme Court fit this mold. It is rare—we hope—for congresspersons to say on the record, as they said while enacting the food stamp law struck down in *Moreno*, that they intended to strike out at certain disliked groups. It should be similarly rare for a city to base a decision burdening a particular group on constituents' fear and dislike of that group, as the lower court suggested the city council might have done in *Cleburne*. And finally, it should be rare for government to impose the type of broad-ranging burden on a group that marked Amendment 2 (struck down in *Romer*) and DOMA (struck down in *Windsor*). Recall that the Court itself stressed how unusual the laws struck down in *Romer* and *Windsor* were; indeed, in *Romer* the Court described Amendment 2 as "unprecedented in our jurisprudence."

Thus the *Arlington Heights* intent factors can channel the animus inquiry, making it less ad hoc than might appear at first glance. This is not to deny that the inquiry remains holistic and impressionistic. It does. But a careful understanding of how the standard intent factors might play out in the animus context gives some hope that the inquiry can be sharpened and made more predictable.

How Stringent Is the Review?

Assume that the inquiry described in the prior section results in a court concluding that, indeed, animus may be lurking as a motivation for the challenged action. Note that the last sentence said "may be lurking" in the action rather than, say, "caused" it. To quickly repeat a point already made more than once, a finding that animus was the reason for a law should end the case. Animus is a constitutional wrong—not a presumptive wrong, not a possible wrong, not a potential wrong that requires a closer judicial look. But all that we know up to now is that the plaintiff, using the *Arlington Heights* factors, has succeeded in raising concerns about the possible presence of animus. In order to determine whether that animus really does exist, a court at this stage of the case should then turn to the government for an explanation.

Usually, that requirement—that the government defendant in an equal protection case bear the burden of explaining itself—takes the form of some form of heightened scrutiny, which is usually described as either "intermediate" or "strict" scrutiny, or other words to that effect. But not in animus cases. As we have seen, none of the Court's animus cases have featured explicitly heightened scrutiny; rather, they feature what the Court simply describes (when it describes it at all) as "rational basis" review.[5]

This failure to be more explicit about heightened rational basis scrutiny has been remarked on, and criticized, by both scholars and judges. There is good reason for such criticism, although addressing that critique would take us far afield from our topic. For our purposes, the challenge becomes to understand how rational basis review can work when it is performed at a higher level of intensity—and, in particular, when it is performed at that more intensive level as part of a search for animus.

One noteworthy thing we can say about at least some of the animus cases is that they insist at all on a government explanation supported by evidence. This is not a normal feature of rational basis review. As the Court has explained it, that review usually allows a court to both hypothesize a legitimate government interest that would have a rational relationship to the challenged classification and to presume the existence of facts establishing that relationship. Thus, when the *Moreno* Court limited its scrutiny of the food stamp "household" definition statute to the interests *actually* asserted by the government and finding at least some support in the legislative history,[6] and when the *Cleburne* Court concluded that it could not find support for the city's zoning decision *in the record*, it appears to have been doing something more than ordinary, extremely deferential, rational basis review.

On further examination, that "something more" is connected in a concrete way to the Court's search for animus. By shifting the burden to the government—to offer a real, not just a hypothesized, rationale for the classification and to produce evidence supporting that rationale—the Court's "heightened rational basis" review seeks to find out, literally, what is actually going on with the challenged action. With the plaintiff having established that an unconstitutional motive—animus—might be lurking in that action, the court in effect turns to the government and asks it to prove that that's not the case. Such proof requires a real (and legitimate) justification for the action, not one that the court itself hypothesizes. It also requires actual proof, not simply a request from the government to the court to "just trust us"—that is, to presume that such facts exist.

These requirements are well crafted for uncovering actual motivations. Quite literally, they seek the real story—the government's real justifications, supported by actual evidence. Note that these requirements do *not* speak to the degree of fit that is required or the importance of the government interest. Under explicitly heightened scrutiny, courts do in fact ask whether the classification fits the asserted interests particularly well—for example, under "strict scrutiny," they ask whether the law is "narrowly tailored" to the government's interest. Similarly, courts applying strict scrutiny insist that the challenged law serve, not just a "legitimate" government interest, but a "compelling" one.

These requirements may, in some indirect way, also aim at uncovering when government is acting for ultimately bad purposes. For example, in the *Croson* case discussed in Chapter 8, a plurality of the Court stated that strict scrutiny "smokes out" invidious uses of race.[7] But because those heightened levels of scrutiny apply only after we know what the government is really doing—for example, strict scrutiny applies only after it has been established that the government intended to classify based on race—such heightened scrutiny aims at a fundamentally different target than the heightened scrutiny that seeks to identify animus. To repeat, the animus inquiry starts from the assumption that we do not know for sure yet what is motivating the government; indeed, it is exactly that question that the animus inquiry attempts to answer. The type of heightened scrutiny that insists on a tighter fit and a more important government interest relates only tangentially to *that* inquiry. The inquiry that relates much more closely to the animus question is the one that tolerates a looser fit and allows government to pursue a less-than-compelling purpose—but only if that purpose is the real one, as demonstrated by actual evidence. This is exactly what the Court insisted on in *Moreno* and *Cleburne*.

It is what the Court insisted on in *Windsor*, as well. As Chapter 5 explained, *Windsor* is unusual in that it neglected to deeply engage the standard questions any equal protection case usually asks: What government interest is (or might hypothetically be) motivating the government, and how closely does the challenged law further that interest? When *Windsor* searched for the presence of animus it did not follow that template. Instead, after identifying the Defense of Marriage Act's unusual features—its breadth and its contravention of the usual federal rule respecting state-law marriage definitions—the Court then proceeded to pronounce that law as based in animus, based on factors such as the legislative history and even the title of the statute. In a sense, after DOMA's breadth and conflict with state-law marriage definitions sufficed to indict the statute in the eyes of the Court, the statutory materials themselves (the legislative history and the title of the statute) served to convict it. And this was all done without giving the defense (that is, the government) more than the most cursory chance to put on a case.[8]

How can we explain this? The dissenters, in particular Justice Scalia, explained it as a Court that was unwilling to confront what they (the dissenters) believed were the plainly legitimate justifications that either did or might have justified DOMA. But perhaps another way to see it is that the prima facie case against the statute—again, the breadth of the burdens it imposed on same-sex couples and its violation of the federalism etiquette under which the federal government normally respected state-law marriage definitions—was simply so strong that it all but established the government's actual (bad) motive. Under that reading, the final set of arguments the Court offered—the arguments about the statute's legislative history—simply provided the smoking gun that the Court was already primed to look for.

This may not strike you as a completely persuasive explanation. After all, Colorado's Amendment 2 was also immensely broad and, in the Court's view, similarly unprecedented, yet the Court in *Romer* still at least paused to consider Colorado's arguments for the law's connection to a legitimate state interest. One might well ask why the Court did not give the same consideration to Congress that it gave to the people of Colorado. Of course, it might be that the people of Colorado *deserve* that extra consideration: After all, as citizen-legislators, the voters of Colorado who enacted Amendment 2 were exercising the most basic right of self-government. Perhaps Congress merits less consideration when its handiwork is challenged.

But whatever the reason, the fact remains that *Windsor*, just like the earlier animus cases, aimed at answering the fundamental question animus doctrine asks: Is the law *really* aimed at burdening a group for its own sake, out of simple disapproval of that group as human beings? *Windsor* may have gotten to the answer more directly. But the earlier animus cases, which got to that answer indirectly, through the heightened rational basis review I have described in this chapter, eventually got there, too. They got there by applying the analogous jurisprudence of discriminatory intent, but in a way that accounts for the subtle, but critical, differences between the two concepts.

This chapter has begun to apply the theory that we constructed in the previous chapters of Part II. I began Part II by explaining in Chapter 6 the deficiencies of an understanding of animus as subjective ill will. In Chapter 7 I then introduced the concept of discriminatory intent, and the *Arlington Heights* factors the Court uses to identify such intent, and suggested that that idea and those factors provided helpful analogies to our animus inquiry. Chapter 8 explained how the concepts differed. Chapter 9 explained how the intent concept—and thus, the *Arlington Heights* factors used to identify intent—could be adjusted to the unique concept of animus. Chapter 10 fleshed out how that adjusted concept answered basic questions about the quantum of animus that should trigger judicial concern and the stringency of the resulting judicial review.

Thus Chapter 10 has built the doctrinal structure based on the blueprints I drew up in Chapters 7, 8, and 9. It is now time to furnish the house, by applying that structure to real-life cases.

11

Applying What We Have Learned

[The intellectually disabled] are . . . different, immutably so, in relevant respects, and the States' interest in dealing with and providing for them is plainly a legitimate one.
—*City of Cleburne v. Cleburne Living Center* (1985)

No matter how one feels about homosexual rights . . . there is a visceral reaction to the obvious implications of gender identity laws. . . . The majority of people will not accept such laws.
—Matthew Staver (2013)[1]

We organize our society around very fixed notions of who men and women are, and people whose very existence challenges that provoke visceral, irrational reactions.
—Chase Strangio (2015)[2]

The challenged laws [prohibiting same-sex marriage] discriminate against a minority defined by an immutable characteristic, and the only rationale that the states put forth with any conviction—that same-sex couples and their children don't need marriage because same-sex couples can't produce children, intended or unintended—is so full of holes that it cannot be taken seriously.
—*Baskin v. Bogan* (United States Court of Appeals, 2014, Judge Richard Posner)

Armed with our new understanding of animus, we can now consider how courts should evaluate claims that a given law is unconstitutionally based in animus. This chapter will consider several different examples of laws that might trigger animus-based equal protection claims. Note something important, however. Even though this chapter focuses on groups or categories, it does so in order to explain how the more granular analysis I have sketched out could be applied to those groups or categories. The analysis remains focused on whether animus lurks in a given decision, rather than on identifying certain groups that merit across-the-board heightened scrutiny. But that more focused analysis takes on different tones depending on the type of discrimination at issue.

Disability

Disability discrimination presents an interesting case study. As a matter of constitutional law doctrine, it is clearly established that disability discrimination receives only rational basis review. There may be good reason for that doctrinal rule: As *Cleburne* noted in the context of intellectual disability discrimination, disability often *is* a valid classifying tool, given the reality that one's disability status often *is* relevant to legitimate government purposes. To be sure, we need to recognize the constructed nature of much disability discrimination—that is, the fact that a "disability" is often "disabling" only because society chooses to create certain situations, for example, buildings without wheelchair ramps, which have the effect of excluding persons we then call "disabled." Despite this important caveat, the fact remains that, at least conceptually, disability classifications are subject to being justified as responses to physical realities. But at the same time, disability, like many other statuses, often triggers feelings of fear and disgust that in turn prompt discrimination and exclusion.

Thus disability presents a situation in which animus as a social phenomenon is potentially present. It also presents a situation in which animus as a legal doctrine is likely an important vehicle for vindicating constitutional rights, given the difficulties inherent in across-the-board heightened scrutiny of disability classifications. These two observations lead us inevitably to *Cleburne*'s two-step analysis—that is, its rejection of suspect class status for (intellectual) disability and its (implicitly) heightened rational basis review, leading to the Court's conclusion about the animus that fatally infected the city's zoning decision. But *Cleburne*'s opaqueness about that second step behooves us to approach animus more transparently.

Let's consider, then, how our approach would analyze a disability classification. First, we should acknowledge the probable shape of any such classification. It is unlikely that a disability classification would impose burdens as broad as those imposed on gays and lesbians by Amendment 2, the Colorado law struck down in *Romer*. Indeed, if a law did in fact purport to exclude the disabled from a whole host of protections, as Amendment 2 did to gays and lesbians, then we would have strong evidence that exclusion for its own sake—that is, animus—was likely afoot. We would know this in the disability context because the very nature of disability discrimination is such that its legitimacy requires that it be tailored to the necessary implications of that disability. For example, we might understand why government could legitimately prohibit blind persons from obtaining a driver's license because blind persons lacked the particular set of capabilities necessary to the function they were being denied the right to perform. By contrast, a broader exclusion of the blind from other functions—say, voting or marrying—would naturally raise the inference that something more invidious was going on.

Thus, in a context such as disability, the breadth of disparate impact would matter in the animus determination. So would unusual departures from the substance or the procedure of the decision maker's actions. Disability discrimination, like many other types of government classification decisions, is usually defended as a justifiable—indeed, technocratic or professional—response to undeniable empirical facts. (Indeed, in *Cleburne* the Court denied suspect class status to the intellectually disabled in part exactly because it considered courts unable to competently second-guess such professional decisions.) To use the same obvious example, denials of driver's licenses to blind persons are justified as the utterly rational response to an undeniable, if unfortunate, fact: One needs to be able to see in order to be a safe driver. Such decisions, as objective, technocratic responses to public policy problems, should not emerge from unusual decision-making processes. Nor should they reflect sudden policy reversals, at least without a good reason (for example, a medical breakthrough, or, conversely, a medical discovery that a particular group of persons presents a previously unknown threat to public health or safety). To the extent the challenged decision reflects such unusual deviations, there is good reason to be suspicious, just as *Arlington Heights* teaches in the related context of the discriminatory intent inquiry.

Let's pause and take stock. Up to now I have suggested that, in order to avoid heightened rationality review, a law classifying on the basis of disability should be, in a word, normal. It should be limited in scope—that is, tailored to the character of the disability, consistent with the ordinary treatment of that disability, and the product of a consistently followed decisional process.[3] As straightforward as this all sounds, it has deep resonance for our intuitions of what constitutes proper treatment of the disabled. Such treatment should be careful, calm, and compassionate—not overbroad, not a hysterical (over)reaction that causes decision makers to reverse themselves without good reason and abandon their normal decision-making processes, and certainly not based on mean-spiritedness or even disgust. To the extent the decision suffers from those latter characteristics, there is reason to be suspicious.

Cleburne provides a case study for our analysis up to now. Recall that in that case the city refused to allow the establishment of the group home for the intellectually disabled, essentially based on two sets of concerns—the actual or feared negative views of neighbors, and concerns about population density, legal liability, and flood evacuation. As we recognized when we examined the Court's opinion in Chapter 3, the second set of concerns sounds reasonable, but the Court discounted them based on the taint created by the first set of reasons. But leave those more obviously troubling red flags to the side. Does our approach to animus doctrine suggest something about the seemingly legitimate concerns for flood evacuation and the like?

It does. Recall that our basic rule about disability classifications is that they should be responsive to the particular challenges posed by that particular disability. Overbroad use of disability as a classification tool—say, to deprive blind persons not just of the right to drive but also of the right to vote—is problematic. But so might *under*inclusive use of disability. Such underinclusiveness— for example, banning a group home for the intellectually disabled based on flood evacuation concerns but not an old-age home or hospital—suggests that it is not the characteristics of the disability per se that are driving the decision. That underinclusiveness might, at least in theory, be enough to prompt a court to wonder whether something else was afoot and, thus, to shift the burden to the government to explain its actions.

To be sure, such underinclusiveness should not always trigger that type of burden shifting. After all, government often classifies in underinclusive ways, and yet in most such cases the Court performs only minimal rationality review. Thus, in the absence of a seriously over- or underbroad classification—the sort of classification at issue in *Romer* or *Windsor*—something else should be required.

Indeed, that something else *was* present in *Cleburne*. Let's bring back into the analysis the first set of concerns I identified above— the concerns about neighbors' likely negative reactions to the presence of the intellectually disabled. In *Arlington Heights*'s terms, those negative reactions constitute part of "the specific sequence of events leading up the challenged decision." Those reactions suggest that something invidious was in fact afoot in the city's decision. They also justified the Court's more searching critique of the underinclusiveness I identified two paragraphs above.

The lessons here are important, if concededly ambiguous—perhaps not surprisingly, given how nuanced animus analysis has to be. First, we need to get a sense of the baseline of "normal," noninvidious treatment in a given regulatory context. In the context of disability, that baseline should turn on the capabilities of the particular group of disabled people—that is, how their disability renders them different from mainstream society. To be sure, and as *Cleburne* noted, making that determination and then applying it to the particular discrimination the disabled plaintiff challenges present courts with significant difficulties. But as a conceptual matter, the first step should be to figure out what qualities actually distinguish the discriminated-against group from the rest of us and how those differences matter in the context in which the complained-of discrimination is occurring.

We can find a distant echo of this first step in *Washington v. Davis*, the 1976 case that announced the discriminatory intent requirement. I have not discussed *Davis* much in this book: Frankly, the opinion is meandering, and it is much easier for us to focus on the *Arlington Heights* case from the following year, which laid out its intent factors in an organized and straightforward way. But *Davis* is useful at this point of the analysis. *Davis* dealt with the District of Columbia's use of a written verbal skills test, Test 21, to evaluate would-be police cadets. Because African Americans were proportionately more likely than whites to fail Test 21, African American plaintiffs alleged that the District's use of the test violated the Constitution.[4] After announcing the intent requirement, the Court proceeded to conclude that discriminatory intent was lacking in the District's use of Test 21.

While *Davis* did not methodically plod through a series of factors to reach its conclusion about discriminatory intent, it did explain that it made perfect sense for the District to seek to ensure that its police cadets possessed a certain level of verbal fluency. As the Court stated: "Test 21 . . . concededly seeks to ascertain whether those who take it have acquired a particular level of verbal skill; and it is untenable that the Constitution prevents the Government from seeking modestly to upgrade the communicative abilities of its employees rather than to be satisfied with some lower level of competence, particularly where the job requires special ability to communicate orally and in writing."

Thus, to the *Davis* Court, there appeared to be a direct relationship between the complained-of government conduct and government's legitimate needs. By contrast, in *Cleburne*, the Court was unconvinced that such a relationship existed. The city cited, among other factors, flood evacuation concerns as a reason for keeping the intellectually disabled out of the neighborhood. But, as the Court noted, that explanation was unsatisfying, given that other residential uses, such as hospitals, presented similar concerns but were allowed in the neighborhood.

To repeat, this lack of fit between the City of Cleburne's exclusionary zoning and its legitimate land-use concerns cannot be enough by itself to establish animus: If such bad fit sufficed, courts would be very busy finding animus in a host of government actions. Thus we need to recognize the second factor *Cleburne* adds to the analysis: the suspicion of bad motives reflected in the lower court's conclusion that the city reached its decision in part because of constituent fear and dislike of the intellectually disabled would-be occupants of the group home. It was that suspicion that led the Court to act on its concerns about that poor fit.

My initial discussion of *Cleburne* in Chapter 3 already made the point that the city's catering to constituent dislike was an important part of its animus analysis. But what our discussion here adds is a sense of how that conclusion fits within the Court's discriminatory intent jurisprudence. *Davis*'s concern that government be allowed to promote its legitimate interests, even if such promotion may cause disparate impact, militates in favor of the government defendant, but only if such challenged decisions do in fact appear to be normal, appropriate uses of that classification tool. In *Cleburne*, that condition was not satisfied, in that the disability exclusion appeared to deviate from the baseline substantive norm of treating disabled persons differently only to the extent their disability actually renders them relevantly different for purposes of the challenged action. And, of course, "the specific sequence of events leading up the challenged decision"—here, the constituents' fear-based opposition to the group home and the city's apparent capitulation to those fears—influenced the city council's decision. That direct evidence of the city's actual motivations was obviously critical, as we might expect it to be, given animus doctrine's underlying concern for ensuring that government decision making is motivated by legitimate, public-regarding goals.

Transgender Status

At the other end of the spectrum from disability lies transgender discrimination. The difference between these two species of discrimination lies, not in any substantive evaluation of the appropriateness or morality of one or the other, but instead in the justifications that often attend such discrimination and, indeed, our very understanding of the two phenomena. As explained in the prior section, disability discrimination is usually defended as an objective, technocratic response to an undeniable reality that a disabled person has a reduced capacity to function in the world. There may be more lurking in such discrimination, but for our purposes one of its basic characteristics is that it usually purports to be a morally neutral response to objective differences.

Transgender discrimination is different. Transgender discrimination often reflects a moral judgment condemning the transgender person. When transgender persons' very existence calls into question the permanence and objectivity of society's binary conceptions of gender they are often viewed, in response, as deviant, morally compromised, or a serious threat to the social order. The severity of the violence that often marks cases of trans bashing suggests just such a visceral response. Obviously, "mere" discrimination against transgender persons lacks this physically violent quality. Nevertheless, at least some instances of that discrimination share with their more violent counterparts a visceral rejection of transgender persons' claim to equal moral worth, as suggested by the quotes at the start of this chapter from advocates on both sides of the issue.

So understood, it is easy to see how transgender discrimination differs from disability discrimination. To be sure, even disabled persons can trigger feelings of disgust that effectively dehumanize them.[5] If such feelings trigger legal discrimination, then such discrimination can be understood as being based in animus. But disability presents a more nuanced picture, at least if we assume, as the *Cleburne* Court did, that some disability classifications respond to real differences and that some such classifications, such as special education programs for the intellectually disabled, are appropriate and, indeed, beneficial. By contrast, it is difficult to see how transgender discrimination reflects anything but social discomfort with the reality of transgender persons.

All of this suggests that transgender discrimination presents a promising candidate for an animus analysis. But it remains to work out how this conclusion can flow through the template this book has sketched out. Again, *Davis* helps us start that process. Recall that in *Davis* the Court refused to accept that the police department was prohibited from employing a test designed to measure communication skills, even if African Americans disproportionately failed it. Underlying that conclusion was a sense that the department's use of the test correlated to a legitimate government goal. If our analysis of the transgender issue is accurate, then such a correlation simply does not exist in this latter context. Instead, such discrimination reflects nothing more than moral disapproval of transgender persons and what they represent.

But we can say more than this. Presumably, any governmental deliberation on, or explanation of, transgender discrimination would feature at least a sizable dose of constituent anxiety. If the very reason transgender discrimination exists is because people are uncomfortable around, or simply dislike, transgender persons or what they represent, then the record of any governmental discrimination on that ground will likely reflect such attitudes. Thus, just as with *Moreno*, *Cleburne*, and *Windsor*, such direct evidence of dislike, disgust, or discomfort should go a long way toward proving the plaintiff's case. It may seem obvious and, indeed, trivial to conclude that direct evidence of animus goes a long way toward proving animus. This objection elicits two responses. First, the *Arlington Heights* Court itself recognized that statements of discriminatory intent by governmental decision makers do in fact help make the case for discriminatory intent. Just because something is obvious does not mean that it need not be stated.

Second, such evidence plays a different role in the transgender context than, say, in the disability context. As in *Cleburne*, direct evidence of animus has the effect of triggering more careful review of the legitimate justifications that might in fact warrant a disability classification. By contrast, if, as we are assuming in the transgender context, there are no such legitimate justifications easily available to the government, then direct evidence of animus should by itself win the case for the plaintiff. Law professors are fond of saying, in the context of academic discourse, that "it takes a theory to beat a theory."[6] In the context of a court's search for animus, we can modify that saying to state that "it takes evidence of a non-animus-based justification to beat evidence of an animus-based justification." Disability, and perhaps other types of discrimination, often feature such non-animus-based evidence. If our understanding of society's reaction to transgender persons is accurate, we cannot say the same about transgender discrimination. The absence of such evidence should thus make it easier for courts to conclude that transgender discrimination reflects nothing but private biases and is thus unconstitutional.

Sexual Orientation

Today, sexual orientation is the issue that most people think of when they think of animus. And with good reason. Animus has been the rationale for the equal protection victories gays and lesbians have won at the Supreme Court over the last twenty years, until the same-sex marriage decision in 2015. The last of those animus-based victories, the Court's 2013 opinion in *Windsor* striking down Section 3 of the Defense of Marriage Act, triggered a spate of lower-court decisions striking down same-sex marriage bans that paved the way for *Obergefell*,[7] with several of those decisions based on an animus rationale. Even more fundamentally, the history of the struggle for gay rights has been largely a struggle against an attitude that gays and lesbians are morally compromised individuals.[8] The turning tide of social acceptance of gays and lesbians has thus been, in part, a tide that has marked those earlier attitudes as prejudiced—that is, as based in animus.[9]

But it is exactly that turning tide that makes sexual orientation an interesting case study of animus doctrine. Whereas fifty years ago homosexuality would have been seen by many Americans as immorality that more than justified being fired from a job, and whereas thirty years ago it would have been seen by many as an undesirable condition from which children should be shielded, and whereas fifteen years ago it would have been seen as fundamentally inconsistent with a home life that merited governmental recognition, today such attitudes are crumbling fast. Thus in the last decade or two the defense of sexual orientation–based exclusionary laws has shifted from morality-based arguments to what I described earlier in this chapter, in our discussion of disability, as technocratic, or instrumental, arguments. For example, contemporary opponents of legislation guaranteeing gays and lesbians workplace non-discrimination rights have largely avoided previous arguments about the undesirability of gay persons as employees in favor of claims that such laws are either unnecessary or unfairly infringe on *others'* rights, such as the conscience rights of employers. Similarly, opponents of same-sex marriage rights have raised a variety of such instrumental arguments, from claims that marriage should seek to protect children, who are alleged to suffer worse outcomes if raised in same-sex households, to arguments that marriage should be reserved to heterosexual couples as a way of establishing marriage as a preferred response to so-called accidental procreation by unmarried couples—which of course is a risk same-sex couples do not experience.

The merits, or lack thereof, of these justifications is something we can put aside for now. For current purposes, what is important is that recent discourse about sexual orientation discrimination has largely, although not completely, abandoned the morality-based reasons that seemed so self-evident not that many decades ago. The recentness of this shift means that we need to think carefully about how a court should respond when government offers instrumental reasons for discrimination that previously had been justified in terms that today we would condemn as based in animus. Should the fact of that shift change the analysis?

Arguably, it should, in ways that speak squarely to the inquiry I have sketched out throughout Part II of this book. The fact that sexual orientation classifications were historically grounded on moral disapproval of gays and lesbians should make us suspicious when now, all of a sudden, more instrumental-sounding justifications are offered as justification for that same type of discrimination. The *Arlington Heights* structure accounts for this argument quite neatly, when it notes as a factor in the intent inquiry the historical background of the challenged government action. In the context of sexual orientation discrimination, that background is troubling, indeed: exclusions from employment opportunities, re-movals of security clearances, and police dragnets designed not simply to catch prohibited sexual activity but also to ferret out and publicly humiliate gays and lesbians who simply chose to congre-gate with each other.[10]

Thankfully, much of this (mis)conduct has passed into history. But the deep-seatedness of that history of oppression cannot be fully and immediately erased by the repudiation of past attitudes and the enactment of anti-discrimination laws. (At any rate, such erasure has not even been fully attempted: No federal job discrimi-nation protection exists for gays and lesbians, and most states con-tinue to lack such protections as well. And much of this erasure has been recent: It was less than fifteen years ago that the last same-sex sodomy laws were wiped off the books.) As Justice Marshall recog-nized in his partial dissent in *Cleburne*, "[P]rejudice, once let loose, is not easily cabined."[11] He made that comment in the course of arguing for suspect class status for the intellectually disabled. But that same insight—that history matters when we judge the fairness of a given type of discrimination—also applies when we perform another version of that same inquiry and ask whether a given in-stance of discrimination is based in animus.

Such suspicion is especially warranted when other *Arlington Heights* factors are present. Most notably, when legislators go on record as stating that they are supporting a discriminatory law because they disapprove of the targeted group or consider it less worthy, there is reason to credit such statements when they are made against the backdrop of this history of disapproval. In *Wind-sor*, Justice Kennedy relied on such statements, concluding that they "demonstrate[d]" that DOMA's burden on same-sex couples married under their states' law was "more than [DOMA's] mere incidental effect" but, instead, was "its essence." Scholars have criti-cized Justice Kennedy's focus on that legislative history, arguing that civil discourse on cultural issues is made more difficult when one side is explicitly accused of mean-spiritedness or bigotry.[12] But when such evidence is considered against a backdrop of already-suspicious government action, we have greater reason to see fire in the smoke of such troubling statements.

Of course, in *Windsor* Justice Kennedy had additional reasons to be suspicious of DOMA, before he cited the legislative history. Recall that he started his discussion of DOMA's constitutionality by noting both the general rule that the federal government follows state-law definitions of marriage and DOMA's immensely broad deviation from that rule, given its wholesale exclusion of same-sex married couples from all federal rights and responsibilities that rest on the status of being married. When earlier chapters of Part II examined how *Windsor* fit within the *Arlington Heights* framework, we observed that such unusual laws fit neatly within that framework's recognition that extreme disparate impact and substantive deviations from normal practice constituted danger signs that the classification in question might be based on animus.

We can now consider that observation, not just in the context of DOMA, but in the context of sexual orientation discrimination more generally. To what extent does such discrimination generally reflect the same characteristics that troubled Justice Kennedy and led him to scrutinize the legislative record as carefully as he did? Some instances of sexual orientation discrimination do in fact reflect concerns that, if not exactly the same as those noted in *Windsor*, are roughly analogous.

Consider, for example, *Stemler v. City of Florence*,[13] a 1994 case from Kentucky. In *Stemler* a federal appellate court concluded that a police officer lacked any justification to arrest a lesbian involved in a DUI incident that featured alleged intimate partner violence against the lesbian's (heterosexual) friend, rather than arresting the alleged batterer who was also acknowledged to have been intoxicated while driving. In a sense this case was easy because the arresting officers conceded that the record supported the plaintiff's claim that the officers singled her out for arrest out of animus toward lesbians.[14] The officers simply asserted that *Bowers v.*

Hardwick, which allowed states to criminalize same-sex sodomy (and which was still good law in 1994), gave government officials a green light to act on animus toward gays and lesbians. Such direct evidence of animus—literally, a concession that the officers acted based on disapproval or dislike toward lesbians—placed this case squarely in the tradition of *Moreno* and *Cleburne*, in which the Court identified government officials' simple dislike of the burdened group (or, in *Cleburne*, their responsiveness to constituents' dislike), as a reason to scrutinize those officials' actions more closely.

Indeed, the government actions challenged in *Stemler* and cases like it,[15] in which officials refuse to enforce laws for the protection of gays and lesbians, implicate several *Arlington Heights* factors. First, they are unusual, in the sense Justice Kennedy recognized in *Romer v. Evans*: The idea that law enforcement officials simply deny one group the benefit of laws, or bring the laws' burdens down more heavily on one group than another, appears, as Amendment 2 appeared in *Romer*, to constitute a literal violation of the command that we are all equally protected by the law. Second, statements such as those in *Stemler*, that the relevant officials discriminated simply because they harbored animus to lesbians, reflect the kind of explicit statements *Arlington Heights* had in mind when it recognized that official statements of discriminatory intent—or here, of the underlying constitutional sin of animus— can be probative. When one combines these factors with the very real, animus-driven discrimination that gays and lesbians have suffered in the past—indeed, a history of such discrimination in the precise context of police enforcement of laws[16]—the *Arlington Heights* factors, as applied to the distinct but related context of animus, clearly cut in favor of finding constitutional violations.

But these cases are the easy ones—they reflect situations in which , literally, the government can offer no good reason to discriminate. In such cases it is easy to suspect the presence of animus. What about cases where the government *does* offer such reasons? One prime example of such a case is *Lofton v. Secretary of Department of Children and Family Services*,[17] decided by a federal appellate court in 2004. *Lofton* considered a challenge to Florida's then-existing ban on gay persons adopting children. The named plaintiff, Steven Lofton, is a pediatric nurse who foster parented a number of HIV-positive infants and, by all accounts (and as conceded by the court), did an "exemplary" job. Yet when he applied to adopt one of those children, the state refused, based on Florida's law prohibiting adoption by gay persons. (Florida did allow gay persons to foster-parent children.) Lofton sued, alleging violations of his due process and (most relevantly for our purposes) his equal protection rights. In response to Lofton's equal protection claim, Florida cited its interests in the well-being of the children under its care. It argued that those children were better off in an environment that featured a marital couple and an environment that featured both a male and a female parent.[18]

The court held that those interests were adequate to uphold the Florida law, based on traditional rational basis review. What is striking about the court's analysis, and what makes it an interesting case study for our inquiry into animus, is that the court did not ratchet up that review to something more skeptical, as the Supreme Court did in the animus case we examined in Part I. Instead, it began its analysis by noting how truly deferential such review can be—how, under most versions of that standard, a court must uphold a law even if, quoting *Romer*, "the law seems unwise or works to the disadvantage of a particular group, or if the rationale for it seems tenuous." The court also observed that, under rational basis review as normally conducted, "the burden is on the one attacking the legislative arrangement to negative every conceivable basis which might support it, whether or not the basis has a foundation in the record."[19]

Given how deferential a standard the court applied, it is perhaps unsurprising that the court upheld the Florida ban. The more interesting question, though, is why the court applied that standard. What made that case different from cases such as *Romer*, where another species of sexual orientation discrimination struck the Supreme Court as potentially based in animus and thus subject to a (de facto) heightened version of rational basis review? Or *Windsor*, where the Court's suspicion of animus led it essentially to ignore rational basis review altogether and scour the legislative record for the direct evidence of the animus that the Court already suspected? What about *Lofton* was different?

Again, the *Arlington Heights* factors might help us understand the court's reasoning. First, Florida's adoption ban, unlike Colorado's Amendment 2, was narrow in scope, touching on only one regulatory area (albeit one that touches on parenthood, surely an important interest). Thus, in *Arlington Heights*'s terms, the law did not have an animus-inquiry equivalent of severe disparate impact—that is, an across-the-board impact on the burdened group. Second, the state provided a neutral-sounding, utilitarian justification for the classification: According to Florida, placement of children in households composed of opposite-sex couples assisted children in shaping their sexual and gender identity.

It is an indication of how quickly public (and judicial) opinion about gays and lesbians has changed that less than a decade after *Lofton* the Supreme Court in *Windsor* was able to cite harm to children as a justification for insisting that the federal government *recognize* same-sex marriages performed by states. (Indeed, it is a further indication of how far public opinion has traveled that Florida's preference for *married* adoptive parents has become essentially irrelevant to its exclusion of gays and lesbians, given the public's embrace of marriage equality.) Nevertheless, for our purposes and from the now-seemingly long-ago perspective of 2004, Florida's argument that children would do better with heterosexual parents provided the *Lofton* court with the same sort of rationalistic, non-morally judgmental justification for the challenged law that I identified as reflecting at least some disability discrimination. Recall what I said earlier in this chapter, in our discussion of disability discrimination. I said that such discrimination should be "in a word, normal . . . limited in scope—that is, tailored to the character of the disability, consistent with the ordinary treatment of that disability, and the product of a consistently followed decisional process." From the perspective of 2004, when the debate about gay parenting was still new enough to society (even if not to gay parents themselves), a law like Florida's appeared intuitively defensible—maybe not necessarily correct, but at least within the bounds of reasonableness. And most important, such a law did not seem necessarily and inevitably based on animus.

Again, none of these observations should be understood as defending Florida's exclusion, even in 2004. And since 2004, the public understanding of the utilitarian merits of the issue—that is, the public's understanding of the scientific evidence on how gays and lesbians perform as parents—has shifted, seemingly decisively.[20] In that sense, *Lofton* has been overruled in the court of public opinion.[21] But still, from the combined perspective of 2004 *and* the rational basis standard, there was enough of a non-animus based rationale supporting Florida's law to justify the court's refusal to find a threat of animus that would in turn trigger the more intrusive rational basis review we saw in cases such as *Moreno*, *Cleburne*, and *Romer*.

But what about today? Is there anything left to any such utilitarian arguments in favor of sexual orientation classification? It seems hard to believe there is. The success of the marriage equality movement—both among courts and with the American people—has had the collateral effect of snuffing out any serious arguments that gays and lesbians can legitimately be excluded from any area of social life. In particular, that movement has succeeded in defeating arguments that, disgust or dislike or disapproval aside, gays and lesbians simply are not good parents or (particularly viciously) untrustworthy as teachers.[22] Even before the marriage equality movement picked up its current steam, few modern Americans thought that there were legitimate reasons to disfavor gays in economic or business transactions: For example, the day had long passed where opponents of workplace equality argued that, somehow, gays were not reliable as employees.[23] The only areas that remained were the military (which Congress resolved in 2011), family and home life, and areas of life implicating children. When the marriage rights movement successfully persuaded Americans that gays' and lesbians' relationships merited the same respect through the status of marriage that heterosexual couples had long enjoyed, it destroyed any utilitarian justification for denying them the same opportunities to be around children, as parents or teachers. With those justifications gone, and with analogous utilitarian justifications for other types of exclusions already consigned to the dustbin, there remains little explanation for exclusions today. Thus, when such exclusions remain, it is hard to see them as based in anything other than simple dislike.[24]

12

Obergefell and Animus

Many of those who believe same-sex marriage to be
wrong reach that conclusion based on decent and
honorable religious or philosophical premises, and
neither they nor their beliefs are disparaged here.
But when that sincere, personal opposition becomes
enacted law and public policy, the necessary consequence is to put the imprimatur of the State itself on
an exclusion that soon demeans or stigmatizes those
whose own liberty is denied.
—*Obergefell v. Hodges* (2015)

On June 26, 2015, the Supreme Court decided in *Obergefell v.
Hodges*[1] that the Constitution protects the rights of same-sex couples to marry. *Obergefell* had been anxiously awaited by both sides
in the same-sex marriage debate. Advocates for same-sex marriage
hoped that the case would mark the triumphant culmination of
the two-decade quest for marriage equality. Conversely, opponents
hoped that the Court would reverse the wave of lower court decisions granting those rights and return the issue to the political
arena, where the impact of the Court's decision might similarly
reverse the political tide that had been moving against them. In
Obergefell the Court made its choice.

Clearly, *Obergefell* was a watershed case in terms of its result.
But for our purposes the case is important for its impact on the
Court's evolving animus doctrine. That doctrine helped set the
stage for the Court's decision. To be sure, the Court relied heavily
on its understanding of due process liberty, as that liberty had been

explained and vindicated in a previous gay rights decision, *Lawrence v. Texas*.[2] However, aside from Justice O'Connor's separate concurrence (discussed in Chapter 4), *Lawrence* did not explicitly address the animus concept, even though the majority acknowledged how the Texas law "demeaned" the existence of gays and lesbians by criminalizing their intimate conduct. But *Obergefell* also relied on *Romer* and *Windsor*, the two most recent sexual orientation animus cases the Court had decided (and the subjects of much of this book's analysis). Indeed, the Court ultimately held that same-sex marriage bans violated due process *and* equal protection. Even more fundamentally, in writing the majority opinion for the five-justice majority, Justice Kennedy intricately interlaced liberty and equality in a way that made those equal protection cases as important as the liberty precedent in *Lawrence*. And with those equality cases came along the concept of animus—albeit in a potentially new way.

Obergefell's Due Process Analysis

At one level, *Obergefell's* analysis is straightforward. After recognizing the importance of marriage as a "fundamental" due process right, Justice Kennedy then explained why the social importance of marriage was promoted, rather than eroded, by the inclusion of same-sex couples into the institution. He noted that marriage was understood as a crucial aspect of personal autonomy, a two-person union "unique" in our society, a vehicle for raising children, and "a keystone of the Nation's social order." Same-sex couples, he concluded, sought entry into the institution of marriage to promote exactly these interests.[3]

How did animus come into play? As we'll see shortly, the Court's animus analysis arose most prominently when the Court turned to the equal protection part of its discussion. But we can already see important aspects of that analysis in the first part of the opinion, focusing on due process. After concluding that same-sex couples satisfy the four reasons he identified as justifying marriage's status as a fundamental right, Justice Kennedy concluded that "[t]he limitation of marriage to opposite-sex couples may long have seemed natural and just, but its inconsistency with the central meaning of the fundamental right to marry is now manifest. With that knowledge must come the recognition that laws excluding same-sex couples from the marriage right impose stigma and injury of the kind prohibited by our basic charter." Thus, the marriage bans imposed harms that went beyond whatever material losses flowed from denial of the right to marry. Instead, they imposed deeper harms: "stigma and injury of the kind prohibited by" the Constitution.[4]

But what did this conclusion say about same-sex marriage opponents? Should we brand them as "stigmatizers," who unfairly or cruelly seek to "injure" same-sex couples? Not so fast. As one might expect from a judicial opinion addressing a delicate culture war issue, one side of which finds its justifications in deeply held religious belief, Justice Kennedy did his best to soften the sting of his conclusion:

> Many of those who believe same-sex marriage to be wrong reach that conclusion based on decent and honorable religious or philosophical premises, and neither they nor their beliefs are disparaged here. But when that sincere, personal opposition becomes enacted law and public policy, the necessary consequence is to put the imprimatur of the State itself on an exclusion that soon demeans or stigmatizes those whose own liberty is denied. Under the Constitution, same-sex couples seek in marriage the same treatment as opposite-sex couples, and it would disparage their choices and diminish their personhood to deny them this right.[5]

We have seen versions of this argument already. Recall *Cleburne*. In that case the Court faulted the city for catering to neighbors' dislike and fear of the intellectually disabled would-be residents of the group home. Recall also *Palmore v. Sidoti*, a case *Cleburne* cited, which we noted briefly in our *Cleburne* discussion. In *Palmore* the Court rejected a family court judge's decision to award a child to one divorced parent, which that judge had based on the rationale that the other parent's interracial relationship would subject the child to harassment. In both of these cases, governmental responsiveness to private biases tarred the state with those same biases and thus rendered the state's action unconstitutional.

Of course, here the private "bias" was not bias at all—at least according to Justice Kennedy. Instead, he described anti-same-sex marriage views as based on "decent and honorable" premises. Still, governmental responsiveness to even such honorable views—that is, enacting such views into "public law and policy"—remained unconstitutional. In the Court's words, such responsiveness "put[s] the imprimatur of the State itself on an exclusion that soon demeans or stigmatizes those whose own liberty is denied."

In this sense, *Obergefell* takes a step beyond *Cleburne* (and *Palmore*). While those cases reject governmental responsiveness to illegitimate private biases, *Obergefell* rejects governmental responsiveness to private views, even "decent and honorable" ones, if they have the effect of irrationally excluding a group from accessing a fundamental right such as marriage. The nature of the right at stake—as fundamental or non-fundamental—is clearly crucial in this analysis. Justice Kennedy began his analysis by acknowledging the fundamentality of the right to marry, which in turn formed the backdrop for his inquiry into whether inclusion of same-sex couples would erode that institution. His conclusion that same-sex couples sought to marry for reasons that promoted, rather than eroded, the institution of marriage then led him to conclude that their exclusion from that fundamentally important institution "imposes stigma and injury of the of the kind prohibited by" the Constitution.

Justice Kennedy's characterization of the harm same-sex marriage bans imposed is telling. He described that harm as expressive ("demeaning" and "stigmatizing") as well as material ("injuring"). It thus went beyond the mere frustration or loss that would occur if the excluded group was the victim of a garden-variety irrational classification—that is, one that did *not* implicate a fundamental right. His use of strong words—"demeaning," "stigmatizing," and (in relation to the children of such couples) "humiliating"[6]— suggests that those laws deem same-sex couples as, literally, less than other citizens. A decision with such effects is unconstitutional because government has no business demeaning and stigmatizing—at the very least, not without a plausible public-welfare justification.[7] This may not be exactly the same as animus. But when we recall that the foundation of the anti-animus idea is the principle that government has no business imposing burdens on persons simply in order to burden them, we can see how a law that "demeans" and "stigmatizes" comes close to one that we can legitimately describe in those same terms.

Obergefell, Equal Protection, and Animus

Our discussion so far has focused on *Obergefell's* due process analysis. But the Court also explicitly addressed equal protection. Given that animus doctrine has largely focused on equal protection, it is important for us to consider the Court's analysis of how states' same-sex marriage bans implicated equal protection.

After engaging in the due process analysis we have focused on up to now, the Court then turned to equal protection. It discussed several doctrinal areas, in particular those relating to marriage, to note how due process and equal protection claims had often informed and reinforced each other. It concluded that analysis with the following observations:

> It is now clear that the challenged laws burden the liberty of same-sex couples, and it must be further acknowledged that they abridge central precepts of equality. Here the marriage laws enforced by the respondents are in essence unequal: same-sex couples are denied all the benefits afforded to opposite-sex couples and are barred

from exercising a fundamental right. *Especially against a long history of disapproval of their relationships, this denial to same-sex couples of the right to marry works a grave and continuing harm. The
imposition of this disability on gays and lesbians serves to disrespect
and subordinate them.* And the Equal Protection Clause, like the
Due Process Clause, prohibits this unjustified infringement of the
fundamental right to marry.[8]

Consider the two italicized sentences, which form the core of
the Court's application of equal protection principles to the same-
sex marriage issue.[9] In the first sentence, the Court recognized
that the demeaning effect of the states' same-sex marriage bans
flowed, at least in part, from the history of discrimination governments had visited on gays and lesbians. In the second, it repeated
its earlier conclusion, from its due process analysis, that those bans
should be understood not simply as "innocent irrationality"—that
is, irrational discrimination that had no particular effect aside
from its denial of the material benefit at issue. Instead, those bans
had broader effects: They "disrespect[ed] and subordinate[d]"
same-sex couples.

In using these two words, the latter of which arguably goes significantly beyond the "mere" "demeaning" he found at the conclusion of his due process analysis, Justice Kennedy echoed the
central idea of animus doctrine. To be sure, he never used that
word in *Obergefell*. But if animus reflects what this book has argued it does—that is, if it reflects the disadvantaging of a group
for no public purpose—then describing a law as "subordinating"
a group comes as close to animus as one can get without using the
word. After all, subordinating a group is the very definition of disadvantaging it simply to disadvantage it—and thus it is effectively
the consequence of a governmental body acting on the "bare desire
to harm" condemned by *Moreno* and the subsequent animus cases.

The Court's equal protection reasoning reveals several lessons
about the state of animus doctrine today. First, it makes clear that

it matters whether a burdened group has been the victim of past discrimination. Until *Obergefell*, one might have been forgiven for reading the animus cases and thinking that such history is irrelevant to animus doctrine. Indeed, as we saw in *Cleburne*, the Court's use of animus substituted for a holding that the intellectually disabled constituted a suspect class—a decision that itself turns in part on whether the given group has suffered from such history. But in determining whether a particular exclusion "works a grave and continuing harm," *Obergefell* expressly stated that history does matter.

This recognition of the role played by larger social reality—here, the long-standing anti-gay discrimination state governments have imposed—points animus doctrine back toward traditional suspect class analysis. Suspect class analysis *always* worried about whether it was a historically politically unpopular group that was suffering discrimination. Animus doctrine, at least up to now, has not—at least not in practice.[10] *Obergefell*, however, made that connection. In recognizing the common relevance of history to both animus and suspect class doctrine, Justice Kennedy has reminded us that both of these strands of equal protection law aim to uncover the same constitutional sin: discrimination that simply harms groups, without advancing the public good. History matters to that inquiry.

Second, the italicized language from the quote above makes it clear, if it was not already, that the concept of animus means more than subjective bad intent. We have seen this already. To repeat a point I have made several times now, the city council in *Cleburne* was not itself accused of harboring dislike of the persons to whom it denied the housing permit; similarly, the family court judge in *Palmore* was not accused of being a racist. Instead, those officials' responsiveness to private prejudices was enough to taint their actions with the stain of unconstitutionality. We have also seen this in *Romer*: Even though the Court eventually concluded that Amendment 2 was motivated by animus, it reached that conclusion indirectly, through a process of elimination, and thus avoided the need to directly accuse the people of Colorado of harboring bad motives.

Windsor allowed the Court to return to the idea of subjective bad intent. But *Obergefell* did not provide as easy a case for finding such intent. *Windsor* involved a challenge to one statute, enacted by one legislature (Congress) whose subjective motivations could at least be examined. By contrast, *Obergefell* considered challenges to several states' laws banning same-sex marriage—and, as a realistic matter, to the laws of every state that had not yet legislatively authorized it. Short of concluding that all of those states had been infected with similar subjective bad intent, it was simply impossible for the Court to reason in *Obergefell* as it had in *Windsor*.

There was also a second difference between the two cases. It was one thing for *Windsor* to reason that the extreme oddity of Congress enacting a broadly applicable marriage law raised justifiable suspicion that something inappropriate was afoot. But *Windsor*'s very observation that marriage was an institution traditionally regulated and defined by states took that argument off the table in *Obergefell*. In other words, if what justified the Court's suspicion in *Windsor* was the fact that it was Congress, not the states, enacting a general marriage definition, then what ground for suspicion existed in *Obergefell*, where the challenged laws *were* state definitions of marriage? All that was left was the realization that, at least for many people in many states, understanding marriage as an opposite-sex union reflected "decent and honorable religious and philosophical premises." How could such understandings reflect the subjective dislike—indeed, what we can fairly call the "prejudice"—that sparked the enactment of the food stamp law in *Moreno*, the housing permit denial in *Cleburne*, and the Defense of Marriage Act in *Windsor*?[11]

The Promise of Dignity

Thus *Obergefell* could not be decided by an easy (if perhaps disrespectful) reference to legislatures' (or constituents') subjective bad intents. Nevertheless, throughout his opinion Justice Kennedy used strong language, describing the same-sex marriage bans as "demeaning," "stigmatizing," "injuring," and "subordinating" same-sex couples and "humiliating" their children. If not subjective bad intent, what could justify that stridency?

As we saw earlier in this chapter, part of the answer lay in the fundamentality of the marriage right. But there may be an additional answer, one that not only connects equal protection and due process but, more relevantly for our purposes, connects animus doctrine with constitutional individual rights more generally. Justice Kennedy cares about dignity. He used that word three times in his *Lawrence* opinion and a full nine times in *Obergefell*. Without taking the time and space to parse each usage, the sense one gets is that, for Justice Kennedy, "dignity" refers to the status one has when one is able to develop one's own personhood as one wishes. For example, he described "intimate choices that define personal identity and belief" as "central to individual dignity." More concretely, he stated that older laws that denied women equal rights in marriage "denied the equal dignity of men and women." Most relevantly to our focus, he wrote that "[t]here is dignity in the bond between two men or two women who seek to marry and in their autonomy to make such profound choices."[12]

Thus, dignity matters to Justice Kennedy. It should also matter to us, as we consider what *Obergefell* contributes to animus doctrine. If, as the above quotes suggest, the idea behind dignity is that it reflects respect for the person as a moral agent, able to make choices that define her own life, then denial of dignity is surely implicit in laws that treat persons as less than equal human beings. As we have seen throughout this book, a common feature of the animus cases is that they feature that denial of equal human status. To be sure, the material deprivations may be major (as in *Romer* and *Windsor*) or they may be by some lights trivial (as in *Moreno*). (To be sure, the *Moreno* plaintiffs who needed food stamps to obtain adequate nutrition may disagree with that last characterization.) But the point here is that common to all the animus cases is a conclusion that the challenged laws deemed certain persons ("hippies," intellectually disabled persons, or gays and lesbians) as proper subjects for subordination and exclusion simply because of who they were. That purpose may have been explicit (as in *Moreno* and *Windsor*), it may have been the impetus behind constituent pressure on government officials (as in *Cleburne*), or it may have been "the inevitable inference" from objective indicators (as in *Romer*). Finally, as in *Obergefell*, it might be "the necessary consequence" of the enactment into law, not of private biases, but of sincerely held religious or moral convictions that have the effect of denying access to something as "central to individual dignity"[13] as the right to share in the advantages of marriage.

Thus dignity has the potential to connect animus, not just with the rest of equal protection law, but with constitutional individual rights more generally. In this sense, animus is a subset of constitutional violations that deal with the deprivation of dignity, in the ways revealed by the cases we have considered and the analysis we have constructed. But it is only a subset. A deprivation of such dignity might also arise from a law that denies *all* persons access to a particularly profound right central to human identity: For example, the Court's reproductive rights jurisprudence speaks in this tone.[14] Or it might arise from laws, like same-sex marriage bans, that deny dignity to some. When this latter type of law arises, a court could simply strike it down as violating the due process rights of the denied group. Alternatively, it could strike it down as violating what *Obergefell* called "the equal dignity" of that group. Or it could do both—as *Obergefell* did. These paths may be different, but it is possible to read *Obergefell* as suggesting that all of them—including the animus path—focus on the promise that all persons enjoy dignity as a matter of constitutional right.

Conclusion

Animus Doctrine Today and Tomorrow

Our search for animus over the course of this book has covered a lot of ground. Temporally, it has ranged from the eighteenth century's idea of faction, to the nineteenth century's class legislation concept, to *Obergefell*'s intricate combination of equal protection and due process in 2015. In terms of subject matter, within the modern era it has ranged from hippies to the intellectually disabled to gays and lesbians. Most notably for our purposes, animus is similarly varied in terms of doctrinal elements, focusing on considerations as varied as subjective bad intent, objective indicators of such intent, and (in *Obergefell*) the vague, but resonant, concept of dignity.

The prevalence of this wide variety of factors might leave you with the impression that animus doctrine is a jumble—that all our analysis has simply left us with scattered walls, floors, and foundations, rather than a coherent structure. But perhaps the better way to understand the Court's current approach to animus is that these various considerations reflect different aspects of the same idea. To stretch our construction metaphor, the Court's current doctrine may best be understood as creating a coherent home composed of different rooms. The rooms are distinct, to be sure. But they are connected. And that connection reveals, in the end, a coherent structure—indeed, a structure that is amenable to future additions.

Different Rooms

Anti-discrimination law is complex, mirroring the phenomenon it seeks to prevent. As the Court's cases have recognized, some cases are easy. Laws preventing blacks from exercising the rights enjoyed by whites present an easy case. As we all know, not all cases are that easy. Is it unconstitutional for the government to prefer the foreign-born children of American mothers over the foreign-born children of American fathers, on the theory that the act of giving birth gives mothers an opportunity to develop a parental relationship that is simply different from fathers'?[1] Is it unconstitutional for a state to require that eye care patients seeking an optician's services in fitting corrective lenses first consult an ophthalmologist or optometrist?[2] Is it unconstitutional for a traffic officer, when confronted with a highway full of speeders, to close his eyes and ticket the first speeder he sees when he reopens them?[3]

Animus cases can be difficult, too. As we have realized, they are inherently granular—the entire reason courts perform animus analysis is that broader-brush analysis (for example, according heightened scrutiny to all intellectual disability classifications) is unsatisfactory. In turn, such granular analysis necessarily emphasizes the particularities of the case before the court. The resulting importance of those particular facts suggests that animus analysis—the approach courts use to determine whether animus is lurking in a given case—will vary.

We have seen this dynamic in the cases we have studied. For example, we saw in *Moreno* and *Windsor* that, when lawmakers explicitly state that they disapprove of the group they are burdening, such statements constitute strong proof of animus. But we also saw that in other cases such statements are less helpful, either because it is difficult to attribute such statements to the governing body (as in *Romer*, where that body was the entire Colorado electorate) or because the challenge is a broader one, encompassing many different laws and thus many different governing bodies (as in *Obergefell*). In other cases the relationship was ambiguous for other reasons, as with the Cleburne City Council's apparent responsiveness to constituents' statements of disapproval.

Other aspects of animus analysis are similarly granular in application and thus similarly variable. Most notably, as Chapter 11 discussed, different types of discrimination reflect different social dynamics, which in turn call forth different applications of the *Arlington Heights* intent factors this book has identified as useful guideposts for the animus inquiry. Indeed, some situations, like the one in *Obergefell*, may be uncomfortable fits with any approach that focuses on intent at all.

The details are intricate, but the basic idea is straightforward: As an approach to equal protection that searches for unconstitutional discrimination at a granular, case-specific level, animus doctrine is incapable of being expressed as a single formula or set of factors, applicable to each case. Rather, each case is its own room.

Connected Rooms

However, those rooms are connected. The different approaches to animus this book identified (in Part I) and explained (in Part II) share the fundamental goal of policing legislation to ensure that it promotes a public purpose, or at least seeks to. The Court's focus on legislators' statements in *Moreno* and *Windsor* provide the most direct evidence on that question. As Chapter 6 noted, however, conceptual and practical problems plague sole reliance on such evidence. Thus cases such as *Cleburne* and *Romer* focused on other factors (such as the constituent opposition to the group home in *Cleburne* and the unusual breadth of the law in *Romer*) as justifications for scrutinizing the challenged action more carefully. As we saw in Chapters 7–9, those factors, and the doctrinal structure within which the Court utilized them, find close analogues in the Court's discriminatory intent analysis. For our purposes what is important about the use of those factors is that they point back to the underlying inquiry in which all the animus cases engage: Does the challenged law seek to promote a public interest?

Obergefell strains our tentative conclusion that the animus cases can be harmonized in this way—that the "rooms" of the animus "house" are indeed connected. (To be sure, *Obergefell* does not use the term "animus," but as I explained in Chapter 12, its conclusions about the stigmatizing and injuring effect of same-sex marriage bans makes it at least a relative of the animus cases.) After all, in that case Justice Kennedy went out of his way to deny any hint that same-sex marriage opponents were motivated by anything we might describe as "bad intent." Scholars have suggested, however, that *Obergefell*'s focus on the fundamental nature of the marriage right, when combined with the discrimination inherent in the same-sex marriage bans, created "stigmatizing" and "injuring" effects on gays and lesbians.[4] Such effects may amount, if not to our intuition of animus as mean-spiritedness, then to the social subordination of a group that is one of the fundamental wrongs identified in the animus cases.

A Coherent Floorplan

The addition of *Obergefell* to our canon of animus (or animus-related) cases brings us to our final question about the current state of animus doctrine: To what extent does that doctrine reflect a coherent understanding of what the Constitution requires? Perhaps counterintuitively, the seemingly rough fit of *Obergefell* with those earlier cases helps us discern a more fundamental coherence in the Court's doctrine.

Recall that a fundamental goal of this book was to tie modern animus doctrine back to the nineteenth-century anti-class-legislation tradition. As we saw in Chapter 1, that tradition is deeply ingrained in American law—indeed, going beyond the idea of equality and extending across a wide range of other areas relating to governance.[5] But that tradition is a difficult one to enforce: Courts performing class legislation review struggled with the challenge of distinguishing between legitimate attempts to promote the public good that required special treatment of particular groups and illegitimate, private-regarding "class" legislation. We saw modern analogues of this same concern when, in cases such as *Cleburne* and *Romer*, we considered the factors that led the Court to scrutinize the challenged discrimination more carefully than normally required by rational basis review.

Scholars reviewing class legislation jurisprudence have sometimes discerned a pattern in nineteenth-century courts' class legislation jurisprudence. In particular, they have identified the fundamentality of the right at issue as a key factor in predicting whether a court would strike such a law down or uphold it.[6] That idea, of course, also lay at the core of *Obergefell's* interlocking due process and equal protection analysis. Indeed, Harvard law professor Laurence Tribe has used the suggestive metaphor of a double helix to describe *Obergefell's* connection of due process to equal protection.[7]

This focus on the importance of the right does not necessarily detract from the core of the class legislation idea as we have come to understand it in this book. The underlying idea of class legislation is that legislatures should not be free to burden groups simply because they wish to (that is, without a plausible public purpose). But that prohibition is in turn founded on an even deeper insight: that such purposeless burdening reflects a subordination of that group—as I said earlier in this book, a burdening of a group for no purpose other than to burden it. Such subordination is even more profound when it relates, as it related in *Obergefell*, to something as important as a fundamental right.

The nature of rights—what they are, and why they matter—is a highly complex legal-philosophical issue that cannot be engaged at this late stage of this examination. But what we can say is that rights are both materially important—that is, they matter for the day-to-day of people's lives—and highly symbolic, in that they reflect what society deems to be the minimum requirements of a dignified life as a citizen. If we understand rights in this (highly simplified) way, we can understand how their unequal deprivation both injures the deprived group and stigmatizes it. It *injures* it by withdrawing the material benefits that right provides. It *stigmatizes* it by making clear to all that that group—and that group alone—is unworthy of the right.

Thus *Obergefell*'s focus on dignity—and, in turn, autonomy to make decisions about one's own personhood—holds the promise of connecting animus with both the rest of equal protection doctrine and constitutional individual rights more generally. At this point, this is only promise, not actuality: Justice Kennedy's soaring rhetoric in *Obergefell* and other cases requires work before it can be understood as a workable doctrine. But that promise exists, and with it, the potential for connecting our animus structure even more securely to the rest of American constitutional law and, thus, solidifying its own rightful place in that law.

Animus Tomorrow

Up to now I have talked about animus doctrine in terms of the house we have built up to now. But how about further additions? Is the floorplan compatible with such extensions?

The first thing we should note is that there may well be a need for such extensions—or, to express it in terms of the doctrine rather than the metaphor, animus may grow in importance in future years. As I noted in the Introduction, American society is growing more and more diverse, as measured by nearly every imaginable criterion. With that diversity comes the prospect, not just of governmental classification ("discrimination," in common parlance), but the type of classification that subordinates—that is, classifications that reflect either an intent to make one group lesser than another or classifications, like the ones in *Obergefell*, that have such severe impacts on one's equal dignity that they have the effect of subordinating.

One might concede this but still wonder why animus doctrine needs to evolve. The reason has to do with the contextualized nature of the animus inquiry, as we have seen in the cases we have looked at. As those cases illustrate, different situations call for different variants of animus analysis. Some may be amenable to a straightforward examination of legislative statements indicating subjective bad intent. Others may require examination of the more objective factors drawn from the Court's discriminatory intent jurisprudence. Others may call, as in *Obergefell*, for an inquiry into the impact of the discrimination on the burdened group's equal dignity. Within these examples there is great room for variation, for example, among the different discriminatory intent factors we have identified as relevant to the animus inquiry and how those factors relate to the dignitary harm the burdened group suffers. Those variations, in turn, create different approaches to the animus inquiry.

The adaptability of that inquiry to different circumstances makes it well suited for twenty-first-century America. As the Introduction noted, the growing diversity of American society raises the prospect of continued social and cultural unease, which will sometimes metastasize into social and cultural conflict. That conflict, in turn, may generate attempts to legislate social hierarchy. We can only guess at the shape such attempts might take. But exactly because those attempts will take different forms and will arise through different avenues, equal protection law needs doctrines that are adaptable. Animus doctrine, as I have explained it, can be one of those doctrines.

Of course, that adaptability can exist only if the doctrine itself appears to observers vague and open-ended. And indeed, animus doctrine can be thus described. Asking the ultimate question about animus—asking, that is, whether a challenged law subordinates a group either intentionally or as a by-product of depriving it of a right necessary to human dignity—requires that we acknowledge the myriad ways in which such subordination can occur. In future cases courts may simply apply a formula from a past case, modify it slightly, or alter it substantially. To the extent those analyses seek to vindicate the ultimate right at stake—the right to be free of government action that targets a group for no good reason—they are legitimate exemplars of animus doctrine. In that sense, they would constitute appropriate extensions to the house we have built.

Finally, animus doctrine echoes the aspirations of nineteenth-century class legislation jurisprudence. Recall, for the last time, that that jurisprudence scrutinized legislative action with the goal of ensuring that no person or group was made the victim of legislative majorities that sought to burden it for reasons that had nothing to do with the public interest. American constitutional law has come a long way since then. Most notably, courts have recognized the futility (and illegitimacy) of second-guessing garden-variety legislation "adjusting" what the Court has described as "the burdens and benefits of economic life."[8] They have also recognized that some classifications—such as those based on race and sex—are inherently problematic. But once we get past those situations, the rules of thumb that courts have used for decades have broken down. A carefully constructed animus doctrine can provide a way for courts to police legislatures' malfeasance without unduly constricting policy makers' flexibility to effect such "adjustments." As such, the doctrinal house we've constructed can not only serve modern imperatives but can do so by echoing deep traditions of American constitutionalism. To return one final time to our construction analogy, the house we have built is, we can hope, not only structurally sound and capable of expansion, but one we can recognize as within the historical tradition of American constitutional architecture.

NOTES

INTRODUCTION

1 For a general discussion of this issue, see Gordon Wood, *The Creation of the American Republic* 53–65, 403–409 (W. W. Norton 1969).

2 *See* Kenji Yoshino, "The New Equal Protection," 124 *Harv. L. Rev.* 747 (2011).

3 *See, e.g., The Random House College Dictionary* 53 (revised ed. 1975) (providing as the first definition of "animus," "hostile feeling or attitude; antagonism").

4 In addition to historical examples of such dehumanization, the philosopher Martha Nussbaum has argued that much of the contemporary bias against lesbians and (especially) gay men flows from a sense of visceral "disgust" at the very idea of same-sex (and especially same-sex male) sexuality. According to Professor Nussbaum, such disgust naturally leads to a view of gay men and lesbians as less than human. *See* Martha Nussbaum, *From Disgust to Humanity: Sexual Orientation and Constitutional Law* (Oxford Univ. Press 2010).

5 Obergefell v. Hodges, 135 S.Ct. 2584 (2015).

CHAPTER 1. CLASS LEGISLATION AND THE PREHISTORY OF ANIMUS

1 Department of Agriculture v. Moreno, 413 U.S. 528 (1973).

2 Some scholars distinguish these two phenomena, identifying more general, but nevertheless favoritism-based, laws as "class legislation" while labeling laws that operate on particular, named parties "special legislation." For our more general purposes, we can lump these two types of laws together while nevertheless recognizing the possibility that this distinction may be valid and useful for purposes of more detailed historical analysis. See Evan Zoldan, "The Failure of Equal Protection and the Alternative of Legislative Generality" (manuscript on file with author).

3 Federalist No. 10 was not the only place where Madison set forth his theory. See James Madison, "Vices of the Political System of the United

States," in 9 *The Papers of James Madison* 345 (Robert A. Rutland et al. eds., Univ. Chicago Press 1975).

4 Federalist No. 10 (James Madison).

5 Barron v. Baltimore, 32 U.S. 243 (1833).

6 It bears noting that, like other fundamental principles of American constitutionalism, the policy disfavoring class legislation can also be implemented by the political branches. A notable example of this phenomenon is the message President Andrew Jackson delivered to accompany his veto of the bill rechartering the Bank of the United States. That message explained that his veto was grounded in large part on the monopoly profits the bank would bestow on a small class of wealthy financiers. In a passage that could be understood as a summation of the class legislation idea, Jackson said:

> Distinctions in society will always exist under every just government. Equality of talents, of education, or of wealth can not be produced by human institutions. . . . [B]ut when the laws undertake to add to these natural and just advantages artificial distinctions, to grant titles, gratuities, and exclusive privileges, to make the rich richer and the potent more powerful, the humble members of society . . . have a right to complain of the injustice of their Government. There are no necessary evils in government. Its evils exist only in its abuses. If it would confine itself to equal protection, and, as Heaven does its rains, shower its favors alike on the high and the low, the rich and the poor, it would be an unqualified blessing.

Andrew Jackson, "Veto Message" (July 10, 1832), reprinted as "President Jackson's Veto Message regarding the Bank of the United States; July 10, 1832," *The Avalon Project: Documents in Law, History and Diplomacy*, at the Lillian Goldman Law Library, Yale Law School, http://avalon.law. yale.edu.

7 Again, some scholars distinguish such "class legislation" from "special legislation"—that is, legislation that singled out named individuals for particular benefits or burdens. See Zoldan, "Failure of Equal Protection."

8 Vanzant v. Waddell, 10 Tenn. 260, 270–271 (1829).

9 Wally's Heirs v. Kennedy, 10 Tenn. 554 (1831).

10 *Id.* at 554, 556.

11 *Id.* at 554, 556–557.

12 *See, e.g., Vanzant* at 270–271.

13 Railway Express Agency v. New York, 336 U.S. 106, 112 (1949) (Jackson, J., concurring).

14 *See* Timothy Zick, "Angry White Males: The Equal Protection Clause and 'Classes of One,'" 89 *Kentucky L.J.* 69, 91 (2000–2001) (citing congresspersons' statements).

15 *See, e.g.*, Eugene Gressman, "The Unhappy History of Civil Rights Legislation," 50 *Mich. L. Rev.* 1323, 1333 (1952) ("In any event, it was the privileges and immunities clause which the framers regarded as the core of section 1 of the [Fourteenth] amendment.").

16 The Slaughter-House Cases, 83 U.S. 36 (1872).

17 *See, e.g.*, Ronald M. Labbé & Jonathan Lurie, *The Slaughterhouse Cases: Regulation, Reconstruction, and the Fourteenth Amendment* 34–42 (Univ. Press Kansas 2005) (noting the connection between the challenged law and threats to the city's water supply).

18 *See, e.g.*, Steven Calabresi & Abe Salander, "Religion and the Equal Protection Clause: Why the Constitution Requires School Vouchers," 65 *Fla. L. Rev.* 909, 958 n. 268 (2013) (citing sources).

19 United States v. Cruikshank, 92 U.S. 542 (1875).

20 *See, e.g.*, The Civil Rights Cases, 109 U.S. 3 (1883) (giving a narrow reading to Congress's power to enforce the Fourteenth Amendment and expressing impatience with continued demands for legal protection of African Americans' equality rights). However, the Court did vindicate African Americans' rights to sit on juries and to be tried by juries that were not selected via racially discriminatory laws. See, *e.g.*, Strauder v. West Virginia, 100 U.S. 303 (1879).

21 Barbier v. Connolly, 113 U.S. 27 (1884).

22 Yick Wo v. Hopkins, 118 U.S. 356 (1886).

23 *Barbier*, 113 U.S. at 31–32.

24 Gulf, Colorado, & Santa Fe Railway v. Ellis, 165 U.S. 150 (1897).

25 Atchison, Topeka, & Santa Fe Railroad v. Matthews, 174 U.S. 96 (1899).

26 Scholars shorthand the Court's protection of this right during the first third of the Twentieth century as "the *Lochner* era," after a 1905 case, United States v. Lochner, 198 U.S. 45 (1905), where the Court struck down a maximum-working-hour law for bakers as violating bakers and their employers' right to contract freely for labor. During that era, courts often—though not invariably—found similar violations in other labor and economic legislation.

27 NLRB v. Jones & Laughlin Steel Co., 301 U.S. 1 (1937).

28 *E.g.*, Erie Railroad v. Tomkins, 304 U.S. 64 (1938) (overruling a century-old precedent providing that, when deciding cases that were brought in federal

court because of the diversity of the parties' state citizenship, federal courts should apply general legal principles rather than the law of the relevant state).

29 United States v. Carolene Products, 304 U.S. 144 (1938).

30 Perhaps surprisingly, the Court hesitated to use political process reasoning when deciding race cases, even though this was the first type of discrimination the Court seriously engaged after 1938. See Michael Klarman, "An Interpretive History of Modern Equal Protection," 90 *Mich. L. Rev.* 213 (1991).

31 This is not to suggest that pre-industrial America did not feature significant regulation. Indeed, as scholars have shown, state and local governments imposed a broad array of regulations during that era. *See, e.g.*, William Novak, *The People's Welfare* (Univ. North Carolina Press 2000). However, industrialization, the decline of small artisans, and the rise of wage labor increased calls to regulate the increasingly complex market.

32 *See, e.g.*, Suzanne Goldberg, "Equality without Tiers," 77 *So. Cal. L. Rev.* 481 (2004).

33 *See, e.g.*, Steven Calabresi & Larissa Leibowitz, "Monopolies and the Constitution: A History of Crony Capitalism," 36 *Harv. J. L. & Pub. Pol.* 983 (2013).

34 *See, e.g.*, Jack Balkin, "Abortion and Original Meaning," 24 *Const'l Comm.* 291 (2007).

35 *See, e.g.*, Victoria Nourse & Sarah Maguire, "The Lost History of Governance and Equal Protection," 58 *Duke L.J.* 955 (2009).

36 Indeed, the modern Court's occasional references to class legislation suggest that the Court might remain open to such a resurrection, if accomplished without the baggage that caused it to abandon that approach in the late 1930s. *See, e.g.*, Romer v. Evans, 517 U.S. 620 (1996) ("Class legislation . . . [is] obnoxious to the prohibitions of the Fourteenth Amendment."). *Romer* is discussed in Chapter 4.

CHAPTER 2. *DEPARTMENT OF AGRICULTURE V. MORENO*

1 Department of Agriculture v. Moreno, 413 U.S. 528 (1973).

2 The brief for the *Moreno* plaintiffs described one additional plaintiff's situation.

3 *Id.* at 530 n. 3 (quoting Department of Agriculture regulations).

4 Technically, the Equal Protection Clause does not apply to the federal government, as it appears only in the Fourteenth Amendment's sequence of restrictions on *states*; however, by 1973 it had been established that the Fifth Amendment's Due Process Clause, which *does* apply to the federal government, includes an equality requirement identical to that in the Equal Protection Clause.

5 *Moreno*, 413 U.S. at 535 n. 7 (abandoned argument) & 535 ("increasing the difficulty").

6 *Id*. at 538.

7 Justice Douglas agreed with the Court's judgment on another ground.

8 *Id*. at 534–535.

9 See Moreno v. U.S. Department of Agriculture, 345 F.Supp. 310, 314 (D.D.C. 1972) (failing to identify the anti-fraud goals as ones that had been or might have been advanced).

CHAPTER 3. *CITY OF CLEBURNE V. CLEBURNE LIVING CENTER*

1 City of Cleburne v. Cleburne Living Center, 473 U.S. 432 (1985).

2 The Court's opinion referred to "retarded" persons. This book updates that usage, except when quoting from the opinion.

3 Scott McCartney, "Quiet Neighborhood Becomes Court Battleground," *Henderson Times-News*, November 22, 1984, at 32.

4 Richard Carelli, "Texas Town Divided over Proposed Group Home," *Bowling Green (Kentucky) Daily News*, May 5, 1985, at 23-B.

5 *See* Dan Bodine, "Proposed Retardation Facility Draws Fire," *Cleburne Times-Review*, August 19, 1980, at 1; Dan Bodine, "Halfway House Filing Suit on Decision," *Cleburne Times-Review*, October 15, 1980, at 1.

6 *See* Bodine, "Proposed Retardation Facility Draws Fire."

7 Carelli, "Texas Town Divided."

8 *Id*. ("I'm a coward," and "The rationale began forming"); Brief for Petitioners in Number 84–468, 7 n. 5 in *Cleburne* 473 U.S. (council members' connections with intellectual disability).

9 *Cleburne*, 473 U.S. at 455 (Marshall, J., joined by Brennan and Blackmun, JJ.).

10 *Id*. at 451 (Stevens, J., joined by Burger, C.J.).

11 William D. Araiza, "Was *Cleburne* an Accident?" 19 *U. Pa. J. of Const'l Law* (forthcoming 2017).

12 In addition to the flood evacuation concern, the city also expressed concern with the sponsoring organization's legal responsibility for the actions of the would-be residents and with the population density of the proposed group home.

13 Palmore v. Sidoti, 466 U.S. 429, 433 (1984).

14 United States v. Carolene Products Co., 304 U.S. 144, 152 n. 4 (1938).

15 *Cleburne*, 473 U.S. at 445–446.

16 This concern arose in other parts of the Court's opinion as well. *See id*. at 442–443.

17 *See, e.g., Palmore*, at 433 ("Private biases may be outside the reach of the law, but the law cannot, directly or indirectly, give them effect.").

18 *See* Araiza, "Was *Cleburne* an Accident?" (discussing the Court's decisional process in *Cleburne*).

CHAPTER 4. *ROMER AND LAWRENCE*

1 Romer v. Evans, 517 U.S. 620 (1996).

2 Amendment 2 reads as follows:

No Protected Status Based on Homosexual, Lesbian or Bisexual Orientation. Neither the State of Colorado, through any of its branches or departments, nor any of its agencies, political subdivisions, municipalities or school districts, shall enact, adopt or enforce any statute, regulation, ordinance or policy whereby homosexual, lesbian or bisexual orientation, conduct, practices or relationships shall constitute or otherwise be the basis of or entitle any person or class of persons to have or claim any minority status, quota preferences, protected status or claim of discrimination. This Section of the Constitution shall be in all respects self-executing. (*Id.* at 624.)

3 Stephen Gascoyne, "Anti-Gay-Rights Law Leads to Colorado Boycott Calls," *Christian Science Monitor*, December 3, 1992.

4 Joyce Murdoch & Deb Price, *Courting Justice* 454 (Basic Books 2001) (quoting Sue Anderson, member of the Board of the Anti–Amendment 2 group "Equal Protection").

5 *See, e.g.,* Linda Castrone, "Amendment 2 Aftermath: One Week Later Colorado Gays Take Stock of What Happens Next," *Rocky Mountain News*, November 11, 1992, at 73; Kris Newcomer, "Gay Bashing Rises Since Passage of Amendment 2, Observers Say," *Rocky Mountain News*, November 9, 1992, at 6.

6 *See* the video of the interview with Angela Romero at 2:25–55 at "Voices of American Law," Duke University School of Law, http://web.law.duke.edu. "Voices of American Law" is an oral and documentary history project operated by Duke Law School, focusing on key Supreme Court cases. *See* http://web.law.duke.edu.

7 "Suicide Note Cites Vote on Amendment: Springs Man Dying of AIDS Said He Couldn't Live in State That Bans Gay-Rights Protection," *Rocky Mountain News*, November 11, 1992, at 9.

8 *See* the video of the interview with Kevin Tebedo at 1:54–2:16 at "Voices of American Law," Duke University School of Law, http://web.law.duke.edu.

9   *See* Jones v. Bates, 127 F.3d 839 (9th Cir. 1997); California Democratic Party
v. Jones, 984 F.Supp. 1288, 1291 n. 6 & 1302 (E.D. Ca. 1997); Gerberding v.
Munro, 134 Wash. 2d 188, 197–198 (1998).

10 This approach does not even address any possible difficulties that grow
out of the attempts of an initiative's proponents to communicate with a
particular sub-group of the population, for example, by targeted mailing or
even targeted placement of online video messages. *See, e.g.*, Derek Willis,
"Online Ads Slow to Catch On as TV Reigns Supreme," *N.Y. Times*, January 30, 2015, at A18 (discussing political campaigns' evolving practice of
selectively placing online ads on the screens of computer users with certain
demographic and political profiles).

11 This material is reprinted in Nan Hunter & William Eskridge, *Sexuality,
Gender, and the Law* (2nd ed., Foundation Press 2011), at 1523–1531.

12 *See, e.g.*, Shawn Mitchell, "A Clash of Rights: Amendment 2 Could Force
One-Sided 'Agreements,'" *Rocky Mountain News*, October 18, 1992, at 127
(making this argument in an editorial in one of the major newspapers in
Colorado).

13 To be sure, many readers today may have no difficulty concluding that at
least some of these justifications—in particular, the immorality of same-sex
intimacy—reflect simple dislike of gays and lesbians. However, the Court
in 1986 had upheld the constitutionality of laws criminalizing same-sex
intimacy—a fact the dissent in *Romer* stressed and that the majority in
Romer ignored. Perhaps more to the point, one reading of the materials
is, not that they called for government to adopt that anti-gay viewpoint,
but instead that they argued that Amendment 2 would make it impossible
for *private* parties to express and act on that view. This distinction can
be overstated: Sometimes, government's failure to protect a group from
discrimination or disapproval can be understood as government endorsing
that disapproval. Considering this question at this point would, however,
take us far afield from my analysis.

14 *See* Evans v. Romer, 854 P.2d 1270 (Colo. 1993) (citing Hunter v. Erickson,
393 U.S. 385 (1969)).

15 *See* Linda Hirshman, *Victory: The Triumphant Gay Revolution* 247 (Harper
Collins 2012).

16 *See* the interview with Angela Romero.

17 *See* "Transcript of Oral Argument in No. 94–1039," Romer v. Evans, at 6.
The attribution of this question to Justice O'Connor is from Murdoch &
Price, *Courting Justice*, at 467.

18 The Court did not explicitly interpret Amendment 2 in this way and stated that it did not need to do so in order to strike it down. It did, however, express doubt about a contrary reading. *See Romer*, 517 U.S. at 630–631.

19 *Id.* at 633.

20 *Id.* at 635. Somewhat relatedly, one prominent scholar writing immediately after *Romer* suggested that the Court had applied the principle underlying the Constitution's Bill of Attainder Clause—the constitutional prohibition on Congress simply decreeing a person to be guilty of a crime. Akhil Reed Amar, "Attainder and Amendment 2: *Romer's* Rightness," 95 *Mich. L. Rev.* 203 (1996).

21 The Court also rejected the state's law enforcement resource conservation argument on the same grounds. *See Romer*, 517 U.S. at 635.

22 The original term "Kulturkampf"—cultural struggle—referred to Prussian prime minister Otto von Bismarck's campaign against Roman Catholicism in the 1870s.

23 *See* Bowers v. Hardwick, 478 U.S. 186 (1986); *see also* Susannah Pollvogt, "Forgetting *Romer*," 65 *Stan. L. Rev. Online* 86 (2013) (criticizing *Bowers* but arguing that its precedential force rendered *Romer's* analysis less coherent than it otherwise could have been).

24 Lawrence v. Texas, 539 U.S. 558 (2003).

25 *See Romer*, 517 U.S. at 644 ("Of course it is our moral heritage that one should not hate any human being or class of human beings. But I had thought that one could consider certain conduct reprehensible—murder, for example, or polygamy, or cruelty to animals—and could exhibit even 'animus' toward such conduct. Surely that is the only sort of 'animus' at issue here: moral disapproval of homosexual conduct, the same sort of moral disapproval . . . that we held constitutional in *Bowers* [*v. Hardwick* (1986)]").

26 *Cf., e.g.,* Kitchen v. Herbert, 961 F.Supp.2d 1181, 1209 (D. Utah 2013) (striking down Utah's voter-enacted prohibition) *with* DeBoer v. Snyder, 772 F.3d 388, 409 (2014) (upholding several voter-enacted bans on same-sex marriage).

27 Steven Smith, "The Jurisprudence of Denigration," 48 *U.C. Davis L. Rev.* 675 (2014). The case, United States v. Windsor, 133 S.Ct. 2675 (2013), is discussed in the next chapter.

28 Edmund Burke, *Speech to the Electors of Bristol* (November 3, 1774), *reprinted at The Founders' Constitution* ch. 13, document 7 (Philip B. Kurland & Ralph Lerner eds., Univ. Chicago Press 1987; online publication 2000), http://press-pubs.uchicago.edu.

29 Indeed, it is telling that judges' and scholars' concern about popular law-making through initiatives has been expressed through the constitutional provision by which Congress guarantees to every state "a republican form of government." Former Justice Hans Linde of the Oregon Supreme Court has been particularly notable in expressing this concern. *See, e.g.,* Hans Linde, "Who Is Responsible for Republican Government?" 65 *U. Colorado L. Rev.* 709 (1994).

30 City of Cleburne v. Cleburne Living Center, 473 U.S. 432, 448 (1985); Reitman v. Mulkey, 387 U.S. 369 (1967). *Reitman* is discussed in Chapter 7.

31 Lawrence v. Texas, 539 U.S. 558 (2003).

32 For a detailed discussion of the facts of Lawrence, *see* Dale Carpenter, *Flagrant Conduct: The Story of* Lawrence v. Texas (W. W. Norton 2012).

33 *Lawrence,* 539 U.S. at 580 (O'Connor, J., concurring in the judgment).

CHAPTER 5. *UNITED STATES V. WINDSOR*

1 United States v. Windsor, 133 S.Ct. 2675 (2013).

2 Throughout the rest of this book, references to DOMA should be understood as references to Section 3 of that law, unless the context makes clear otherwise.

3 Ariel Levy, "The Perfect Wife," *New Yorker,* September 20, 2013.

4 The Dutch law was enacted in late 2000 and took effect in 2001.

5 *Windsor,* 133 S.Ct. at 2692 (2013).

6 *Id.* at 2696.

7 *Id.* at 2694.

8 *Id.* at 2708.

9 The use of this term to describe animus is from Susannah Pollvogt.

CHAPTER 6. WHAT'S WRONG WITH SUBJECTIVE DISLIKE?

1 Public Law 42–32, 17 Stat. 13.

2 Griffin v. Breckenridge, 403 U.S. 88, 102 (1971).

3 Bray v. Alexandria Women's Health Clinic, 506 U.S. 263 (1993). In *Griffin* the Court had hedged on the question whether the required animus could be based on something other than race. *Bray* did not answer that question, since it stated that the plaintiffs had not demonstrated any other type of class-based animus.

4 *Bray,* 506 U.S. at 269–270 (emphasis in original).

5 In *Bray,* for example, the Court understood such "objectively invidious" intent to include a romantic paternalism that prevented women from entering occupational fields that were deemed inappropriately "aggressive" for them.

6 Frank Easterbrook, "Some Tasks in Understanding Law through the Lens of Public Choice," 12 *Int'l Rev. of Law & Econ.* 284 (1992).

7 LeClair v. Saunders, 627 F.2d 606 (2nd Cir. 1980).

8 Village of Willowbrook v. Olech, 528 U.S. 562 (2000).

9 Geinosky v. Chicago, 675 F.3d 743 (7th Cir. 2012).

10 To be sure, in its first encounter with the class-of-one theory the Court expressly rejected the argument that subjective ill will was a necessary part of a class-of-one claim. *See Olech*, 528 U.S. at 565. Justice Breyer expressed concern with the Court's view on this point. *See id.* at 565 (Breyer, J., concurring in the result). Perhaps even more tellingly, though, lower courts after *Olech* often continued to insist that class-of-one plaintiffs demonstrate such ill will—if not as a matter of constitutional law, then at least as a matter of providing adequate proof to withstand a defendant's summary judgment motion. *See, e.g.,* William D. Araiza, "Constitutional Rules and Institutional Roles: The Fate of the Equal Protection Class of One and What It Means for Congressional Power to Enforce Constitutional Rights," 62 *SMU L. Rev.* 27, 53 (2009).

11 The constitutional requirement that Congress keep a "journal" of its proceedings may reflect an expectation that congressional members would record the reasons for their votes—and perhaps an implied requirement that they do so. Thanks to Evan Zoldan for this insight.

12 *See* the discussion in Chapter 4 of this book.

13 McCleskey v. Kemp, 481 U.S. 279, 296 (1987).

CHAPTER 7. OBJECTIVELY OBJECTIONABLE

1 Washington v. Davis, 426 U.S. 229 (1976).

2 Some scholars have suggested that the Court's later pronouncements on the intent requirement have at times (although not consistently) sharpened the intent requirement into an insistence that the plaintiff prove the actual, subjective intent of government decision makers, thus creating ambiguity with regard to the meaning of "discriminatory intent." *See, e.g.,* Sheila Foster, "Intent and Incoherence," 72 *Tulane L. Rev.* 1065, 1084–1085 (1998); Ian Haney-Lopez, "Intentional Blindness," 87 *N.Y.U. L. Rev.* 1779 (2012). For our purposes we do not need to enter the debate into how the Court's discriminatory intent jurisprudence has evolved since *Arlington Heights* (Village of Arlington Heights v. Metropolitan Housing Development Corp. 429 U.S. 252 (1977)). Instead, we can assume that the Court's intent jurisprudence does in fact allow for a more holistic, "constructed" intent, rather than insisting on a narrower understanding focusing on the

subjective will of the government decision maker. This assumption serves our purpose of using the Court's original understanding of intent doctrine to craft an analogous animus doctrine, even if that original understanding has changed. Indeed, if that understanding has changed, then there may be room to argue that the Court's approach to animus is inconsistent with that evolution and, thus, raises questions about the correctness of that evolution.

3   Gomillion v. Lightfoot, 364 U.S. 339 (1960).

4   *Id.* at 341.

5   See Personnel Administrator of Massachusetts v. Feeney, 442 U.S. 256 (1979) (rejecting the argument that the foreseeability of a law's disparate impact establishes that the legislature necessarily acted intentionally); *id.* at 279 n. 25 (recognizing that such foreseeability remains relevant to the issue of the legislature's intent).

6   Village of Arlington Heights v. Metropolitan Housing Development Corp., 429 U.S. 252 (1977).

7   *Id.* at 266–268.

8   *See* Anatole France, *The Red Lily* (Le lys rouge) 95 (W. Stephens trans. 6th ed., Dodd, Mead 1922).

9   Griffin v. County School Board of Prince Edward County, 377 U.S. 218, 229 (1964). The Court's references to "deliberation" and "speed" are to its decision in the follow-on case to Brown v. Board of Education (347 U.S. 483 (1954)), where the Court directed that local school districts act with "all deliberate speed" to desegregate their schools (Brown v. Board of Education, 349 U.S. 294 (1955). The Court issued that mandate in 1955, a decade before its decision in *Griffin*.

10   Reitman v. Mulkey, 387 U.S. 369 (1967).

11   It had earlier applied the disparate impact factor, noting that the town's rejection of the housing project would affect racial minorities more than whites. It had also noted the long-standing nature of the town's zoning policy.

12   *See, e.g.,* Siobhan Somervile, "Scientific Racism and the Emergence of the Homosexual Body," 5 *J. Hist. Sexuality* 243 (1994).

13   *See Arlington Heights*, 429 U.S. at 257–258.

14   Indeed, one commentator has criticized what she views as the *overly* focused nature of this inquiry. See Sofia Martos, "Coded Codes: Discriminatory Intent, Modern Political Mobilization, and Local Immigration Ordinances," 85 *N.Y.U. L. Rev.* 2099 (2010).

15   *Arlington Heights*, 429 U.S. at 269.

16 *See* Dan Bodine, "Proposed Retardation Facility Draws Fire," *Cleburne Times-Review*, August 19, 1980.

17 *See* Richard Carelli, "Texas Town Divided over Proposed Group Home," *Bowling Green (Kentucky) Daily News*, May 25, 1985.

18 Justice Stevens did not participate in the case. Justice Marshall, joined by Justice Brennan, concurred in part, and in particular agreed with the majority's enumeration of those factors. He disagreed, though, with the majority's decision to apply those factors to the case before it; instead, he would have remanded the case to the lower court for it to apply those factors in the first instance. Perhaps ironically, it was Justice White, the author of Washington v. Davis, who dissented. But even he did not disagree with those factors on their own merits; instead, he would have remanded the case to the lower court for it to apply *Davis*'s holding as it thought best, since the lower court had decided the case before *Davis* was decided.

CHAPTER 8. THE DOCTRINAL UNIQUENESS OF ANIMUS

1 Grutter v. Bollinger, 539 U.S. 306 (2003); Fisher v. University of Texas at Austin, 136 S.Ct. 2198 (2016).

2 City of Richmond v. J. A. Croson Co., 488 U.S. 469 (1989).

3 A careful reader might note that the Michigan, Texas, and Richmond cases involved situations in which the government's use of race was apparent on its face—that is, they did not involve situations in which an ostensibly neutral law was found to have been motivated by an intent to classify on the challenged ground. But this distinction does not make a difference for our purposes. The cases discussed in the text make clear that not all government use of race is necessarily unconstitutional. Whether that use of race was explicit, as in the Michigan, Texas, and Richmond cases, or covert is technically irrelevant to this point.

   To be sure, overt discrimination may (ironically) be more easily defensible as a practical matter. This might be the case because race and sex discrimination demand such convincing justifications that it might be difficult for the government to begin by denying that it had discriminated on that ground and then, after being rebuffed, pivoting and suddenly providing compelling justifications for exactly that type of discrimination. Nevertheless, the formal structure of the inquiry does not turn on whether the discrimination is facial or covert.

4 City of Cleburne v. Cleburne Living Center, 473 U.S. 432, 450 (1985).

5 *See* Timothy Zick, "Angry White Males: The Equal Protection Clause and 'Classes of One,'" 89 *Kentucky L.J.* 69, 91 (2000–2001).

6 United States v. Carolene Products, 304 U.S. 144 (1938). Justice Lewis Powell once called Footnote 4 "the most celebrated footnote in constitutional law." Lewis Powell, "*Carolene Products* Revisited," 82 *Columbia L. Rev.* 1087 (1982).

7 *See, e.g.,* United States v. Windsor, 133 S.Ct. 2675, 2716 (2013) (Alito, J., dissenting) ("The modern tiers of scrutiny . . . are a heuristic to help judges determine when classifications have [the] fair and substantial relation to the object of the legislation" that is "the central notion" of equal protection jurisprudence.).

8 *See* Richard H. Fallon, Jr., *Implementing the Constitution* 61 (Harvard Univ. Press 2001) ("[T]he American constitutional tradition has long recognized a judicial authority, not necessarily linked to any specifically enumerated guarantee, to invalidate truly arbitrary legislation.").

9 Most notably, Justice Stone wrote a letter to Judge Irving Lehman the day after *Carolene Products* was decided, expressing concern about the growing racial and ethnic intolerance in the world. *See* Alpheus Thomas Mason, *Harlan Fiske Stone, Pillar of the Law* 515 (Viking 1956).

10 *See, e.g.,* Graham v. Richardson, 403 U.S. 365 (1971) (alienage); Mathews v. Lucas, 427 U.S. 495 (1976) (legitimacy). Not all of these considerations resulted in a grant of suspect class status. *See, e.g.,* Massachusetts Board of Retirement v. Murgia, 427 U.S. 307 (1976) (rejecting heightened scrutiny for age discrimination); *Cleburne* (rejecting such scrutiny for intellectual disability discrimination).

11 *See Cleburne,* 473 U.S. at 450 ("The short of it is that requiring the permit in this case appears to us to rest on an irrational prejudice against the mentally retarded.").

12 City of Richmond v. J. A. Croson Co., 488 U.S. 469 (1989).

13 *Id.* at 493.

14 *See, e.g.,* Fullilove v. Klutznick, 448 U.S. 448 (1980) (Stevens, J., dissenting) (describing the efforts of a group of congresspersons to ensure that their constituents received "a piece of the action" via a race-based set-aside for federal construction projects).

15 Department of Agriculture v. Moreno, 413 U.S. 528, 534–535 (1973) (second set of italics added).

16 Susannah Pollvogt, "Unconstitutional Animus," 81 *Fordham L.Rev.* 887, 904 (2012).

17 *Id.* at 930; emphasis added.

18 Dale Carpenter, "*Windsor* Products: Equal Protection from Animus," 2013 *Supreme Court Review* 183, 232.

CHAPTER 9. THE ELUSIVE SEARCH FOR ANIMUS

1 As I have already noted, sometimes such disparate impact may be so severe as to be, in the Court's words, "unexplainable on grounds other than" the ground on which that disparate impact exists (for example, race). *See* Village of Arlington Heights v. Metropolitan Housing Development Corp. 429 U.S. 252, 266 (1977). We can leave this detail aside.

2 Analogous, although not identical, burden shifting has long been a principle of federal statutory employment non-discrimination law. *See* McDonnell Douglas Corp. v. Green, 411 U.S. 792 (1973).

3 To be sure, many scholars resist this assumption. For example, one strand of academic thinking maintains that denials of equal protection consist not just of intentional deprivations of equal treatment but also of governmental failures to actively consider the interests of particular groups when making decisions. Such failures may not be describable as "intentional" discrimination in the sense *Davis* (Washington v. Davis, 426 U.S. 229 (1976)) and *Arlington Heights* assume. The correctness of this and other approaches to equal protection is far beyond the scope of this book, which takes the intent requirement as a given and builds an animus doctrine consistent with it.

4 Again, this statement assumes the correctness of the intent requirement. Many scholars resist this assumption. *See supra* note 3.

5 Personnel Administrator of Massachusetts v. Feeney, 442 U.S. 256; 279 (1979).

6 *See, e.g.*, Grutter v. Bollinger, 539 U.S. 306 (2003) (upholding the University of Michigan Law School's use of race in its admissions decisions).

7 Daniel Conkle, "Evolving Values, Animus, and Same-Sex Marriage," 89 *Ind. L.J.* 27 (2014) ("insulting and disrespectful"); Steven Smith, "The Jurisprudence of Denigration," 48 *U.C. Davis L.Rev.* 675 (2014). *See also* Brief of *Amici Curiae* Steven G. Calabresi, Daniel O. Conkle, Michael J. Perry, and Brett G. Scharffs in Support of Certiorari and Opposing a Ruling Based on Voters' Motivations in No. 14–124, Kitchen v. Herbert, 2014 WL 4380924, at 2 (urging the Supreme Court to grant review in a same-sex marriage case in order to hold that voter-enacted same-sex marriage bans are not based in animus, an accusation the *amici* described as "unfair" and one that "violates the integrity and aspirations of our shared political discourse"). Similarly, another prominent scholar, defending the Court's result in the 2015 case striking down *state*-law same-sex marriage bans, felt compelled to defend the Court against the

claim that it was accusing same-sex marriage opponents of acting out of "bigotry." Carlos Ball, "Bigotry and Same-Sex Marriage," 84 *UMKC L. Rev.* 3 (2016).

8 Romer v. Evans, 517 U.S. 620, 636 (1996) (Scalia, J., dissenting).

9 United States v. Windsor, 133 S.Ct. 2675, 2708 (Scalia, J., dissenting).

10 *See* Price Waterhouse v. Hopkins, 490 U.S. 228 (1989) (plurality opinion) (accepting the argument that "sex discrimination" in federal employment discrimination law includes discrimination based on gender stereotyping).

CHAPTER 10. HOW MUCH ANIMUS IS ENOUGH? AND WHAT SHOULD WE DO ABOUT IT?

1 Rogers v. Lodge, 458 U.S. 613 (1982).

2 Reitman v. Mulkey, 387 U.S. 369 (1967).

3 Village of Arlington Heights v. Metropolitan Housing Development Corp. 429 U.S. 252, 270 (1977).

4 Indeed, it is worth noting that the Court cast its conclusion about intent in terms of whether "the evidence . . . warrant[s] overturning" the lower court's "findings" about intent. Leaving aside the implication that an intent "finding" is fundamentally factual, the Court's language casting its decision as one where the evidence did not warrant overturning those lower court findings suggests that the intent question is one whose answer is primarily entrusted to the trial court that hears the evidence most directly and can thus weigh it most accurately. *Id.* at 270.

5 To be sure, Justice O'Connor's concurrence in *Lawrence* (Lawrence v. Texas, 539 U.S. 558 (2003)) did describe the Court's approach in these cases as implementing heightened rationality review. But the majority opinions she described did not themselves do so.

6 The government's Supreme Court brief in *Moreno* cited statements by congresspersons expressing concern over fraud perpetrated by unrelated persons cohabiting and living off food stamps. *See* Brief for the Appellants in No. 72-534, U.S. Department of Agriculture v. Moreno, 1973 WL 173826, at 15–16.

7 City of Richmond v. J. A. Croson Co., 488 U.S. 469, 493 (1989) (plurality opinion). The full quote is provided at the start of Chapter 8.

8 Recall from Chapter 5 that the Court did, at the end of its opinion, state, without analysis, that no legitimate interest "overcame" the injuries DOMA intentionally imposed.

CHAPTER 11. APPLYING WHAT WE HAVE LEARNED

1 Matthew Staver is the counsel for Liberty Counsel, a conservative litigation and policy organization. The quotation comes from "Many Hurdles Ahead for Transgender Rights Movement," *USA Today Online*, December 14, 2013, www.usatoday.com.

2 Chase Strangio is a lawyer for the American Civil Liberties Union who focuses on lesbian, gay, bisexual, and transgender issues. The quotation comes from Deborah Sontag, "Once a Pariah, Now a Judge: The Early Transgender Journey of Phyllis Frye," *N.Y. Times*, August 29, 2015, www.nytimes.com.

3 For a roughly analogous statement from an important constitutional law treatise of the police power era, see Thomas M. Cooley, *A Treatise on the Constitutional Limitations Which Rest upon the Legislative Power of the States of the American Union* 16–17 (1st ed., Little, Brown 1868) ("[T]here may be discriminations between classes of persons where reasons exist which make them necessary or advisable," such as laws establishing an age of majority and barring minors from entering into contracts, "but no one would undertake to defend upon constitutional grounds an enactment that, of the persons reaching that age, those possessing certain physical characteristics, in no way affecting their capacity or fitness for general business or impairing their usefulness as citizens, should remain in a condition of permanent disability.").

4 Because the District of Columbia is a federal government institution, the claim was brought under the Fifth Amendment's Due Process Clause, rather than the Fourteenth Amendment's Equal Protection Clause, the latter of which applies to states but not the District of Columbia. But the Court has understood the former, which *does* apply to the federal government, to include an equality component equal in scope and content to the Equal Protection Clause.

5 *See, e.g.*, Constantina Safilios-Rothschild, "Prejudice against the Disabled and Some Means to Combat It," in *Social and Psychological Aspects of Disability* 261, 265 (Joseph Stubbins ed., University Park Press 1977).

6 *See* Lawrence Solum, "Legal Theory Lexicon: It Takes a Theory to Beat a Theory," *Legal Theory Blog*, October 21, 2012, http://lsolum.typepad.com.

7 In *Obergefell* (Obergefell v. Hodges, 135 S.Ct. 2584 (2015)), Justice Kennedy rejected the dissenters' call for more public debate on same-sex marriage, noting in part the wave of same-sex marriage cases that were decided after *Windsor* (United States v. Windsor, 133 S.Ct. 2675 (2013)), many of which relied on *Windsor*'s reasoning.

8 For an example of one commentator's personal reflection on his experience of such feelings, *see* Frank Bruni, "Sex, Lies, and Houston," *N.Y. Times,* November 8, 2015, Sunday Review section, at 3, www.nytimes.com.

9 Indeed, in his *Romer* dissent Justice Scalia remarked on the battle over how to understand anti-gay opinion, arguing that it should be fought exclusively in the political and social arena rather than through constitutional litigation (even if Amendment 2 made that fight much harder for one side by enshrining the other side's position in the state constitution). *See* Romer v. Evans, 517 U.S. 620, 646 (1996) (Scalia, J., dissenting).

10 *See, e.g.,* Christopher Leslie, "Creating Criminals: The Injuries Inflicted by 'Unenforced' Sodomy Laws," 35 *Harv. Civ. Rights-Civ. Liberties L. Rev.* 103, 154–156 (2000).

11 City of Cleburne v. Cleburne Living Center, 473 U.S. 432, 464 (1985).

12 *See, e.g.,* Steven Smith, "The Jurisprudence of Denigration," 48 *U.C. Davis L. Rev.* 675 (2014).

13 Stemler v. City of Florence, 126 F.3d 856 (6th Cir. 1997).

14 The wording in this sentence matters because this case came to the court "on the pleadings"—that is, before there had been a definitive determination of the actual facts.

15 *E.g.,* Price-Cornelison v. Brooks, 524 F.3d 1103 (10th Cir. 2008) (holding that a lesbian had adequately alleged that the local police has a policy of not enforcing protective orders benefiting lesbian victims of domestic violence and that, if proven, the existence of such a policy would violate equal protection).

16 Leslie, "Creating Criminals."

17 Lofton v. Secretary of Department of Children and Family Services, 358 F.3d 804 (11th Cir. 2004).

18 Given that this case arose in the mid-1990s and was decided in 2004, when only Massachusetts had instituted same-sex marriage, and given that Lofton did not challenge Florida's marriage ban, it is unsurprising that Florida cited the marital preference as well as the mother/father preference.

19 *Id.* at 818 (quoting Heller v. Doe, 509 U.S. 312, 320–321 (1993)).

20 Art Swift, "Most Americans Say Same-Sex Couples Entitled to Adopt," poll, May 30, 2014, www.gallup.com (finding that, as of 2014, 63 percent of Americans thinks same-sex couples should be allowed to adopt children, as compared with 28 percent in 1994).

21 A state court, relying on *state* constitutional equality grounds, ultimately struck down the law. Florida Department of Children and Families v.

Adoption of X.X.G., 45 So.3d 79 (Fla. App. 2010). Thanks to Katie Eyer for pointing this out.

22 See Bruni, "Sex, Lies, and Houston."

23 *See, e.g.,* Lauren Fox, "GOP Leaders Still Oppose ENDA," *U.S. News and World Report,* June 16, 2014, www.usnews.com (noting House Republican leadership's opposition to employment non-discrimination legislation for gays and lesbians on the grounds that it is "unnecessary" and "would provide a basis for frivolous lawsuits"). For polling suggesting that a majority of Americans have supported workplace non-discrimination for decades, see Gallup, "Gay and Lesbian Rights," poll, n.d., www.gallup.com.

24 To be sure, such dislike or disapproval might warrant legal protection to the extent those feelings are themselves constitutionally protected—most notably, as expressions of religious faith. Hence, it is not surprising to see that the battleground over gay rights has in fact largely shifted to the scope of the law's recognition of such religiously based moral disapproval.

CHAPTER 12. *OBERGEFELL* AND ANIMUS

1 Obergefell v. Hodges, 135 S.Ct. 2584 (2015).

2 Lawrence v. Texas, 539 U.S. 558 (2003). *Lawrence* is discussed in Chapter 4.

3 *Obergefell,* 135 S.Ct. at 2594 ("unique") & 2601 ("keystone").

4 *Id.* at 2602.

5 *Id.*

6 Justice Kennedy first used this description in *Windsor. See* United States v. Windsor, 133 S.Ct. 2675, 2694 (2013).

7 Justice Kennedy acknowledged a primary public-welfare argument made by defenders of same-sex marriage bans: that restricting marriage to opposite-sex couples was necessary in order to encourage such couples to marry when they accidentally procreated. But, echoing much of the lower court reaction to this argument, he dismissed it, observing that excluding same-sex couples from marriage had no effect on the willingness of such "accidentally procreating" couples to wed.

8 *Obergefell,* 135 S.Ct. at 2604 (emphasis added).

9 To be sure, the previous sentence evokes the "fundamental rights strand" of equal protection, in which a discriminatory denial of a fundamental right is subjected to careful scrutiny. This analysis is, in some ways, simply another version of the due process analysis the Court had performed in the previous part of its opinion. *See, e.g.,* Erwin Chemerinsky, *Constitutional Law: Principles and Policies* 793 (3rd ed., Aspen 2006) ("Relatively little

depends on whether the Court uses due process or equal protection as the basis for protecting a fundamental right.").

10　Of course, the foundational statement of animus doctrine—*Moreno*'s statement that "a bare . . . desire to harm *a politically powerless* group" cannot serve as a legitimate government interest—does speak, explicitly so, to political powerlessness (Department of Agriculture v. Moreno, 413 U.S. 528, 534 (1973)). But in practice, the Court has not explicitly focused on a group's political powerlessness or its components, such as its history of discrimination, when applying that statement.

11　Indeed, one scholar has seen fit to attempt to rebut the argument that the *Obergefell* Court accused same-sex opponents of bigotry. See Carlos Ball, "Bigotry and Same-Sex Marriage," 84 *UMKC L. Rev.* 3 (2016).

12　*Obergefell*, 135 S.Ct. at 2597 ("intimate choices"), 2603 ("men and women"), & 2599 ("dignity in the bond").

13　*Id.* at 2597.

14　Indeed, in *Lawrence* Justice Kennedy quoted the portion of the seminal modern abortion rights case, Planned Parenthood v. Casey (505 U.S. 833 (1992)), which used "dignity" to characterize rights central to one's personhood. Similarly, in *Obergefell* he described cases dealing with access to contraception as dealing with similarly important rights.

CONCLUSION

1　Nguyen v. INS, 533 U.S. 53 (2001).

2　Williamson v. Lee Optical, 348 U.S. 483 (1955).

3　*See* Oregon Department of Agriculture v. Engquist, 553 U.S. 591; 603–604 (2008) (considering a similar hypothetical).

4　*See, e.g.,* Kenji Yoshino, "The Supreme Court 2014 Term—Comment: A New Birth of Freedom?: *Obergefell v. Hodges,*" 129 *Harv. L. Rev.* 147 (2015); Laurence Tribe, "Equal Dignity: Speaking Its Name," 129 *Harv. L. Rev. F.* 16 (2015).

5　*See* Evan Zoldan, "Reviving Legislative Generality," 98 *Marquette L. Rev.* 625 (2014).

6　*See* Victoria Nourse & Sarah Maguire, "The Lost History of Governance and Equal Protection," 58 *Duke L.J.* 955, 983 (2009).

7　*See* Tribe, "Equal Dignity."

8　Usery v. Turner Elkhorn Mining Co., 428 U.S. 1, 15 (1976).

ABOUT THE AUTHOR

After graduating from Yale Law School, William D. Araiza clerked on the Ninth U.S. Circuit Court of Appeals and for Justice David Souter of the United States Supreme Court. Araiza has published widely in administrative and constitutional law and is Vice Dean and Professor of Law at Brooklyn Law School.

Lightning Source UK Ltd.
Milton Keynes UK
UKOW03n0312240217
295214UK00009B/100/P